Praise for *Min*

In a world in which media, news and others are telling you what to think, *Mindset Medicine* is a powerful tool to regain your consciousness. We all have an Innate power within us, a power wanting to be expressed and live fully. This book will draw that out. Enjoy with an open mind and let your mind be refreshed into a higher level of health and consciousness.

– Dr. Aaron Tressler, Chiropractor,
Podcaster and Critical Thinker

Mindset Medicine doesn't merely inspire you to transform how you view yourself and your life; it teaches you how. This book, filled with journaling prompts, will reshape your outlook from a societally-imposed "should" mindset to one of exciting, self-driven possibility. Mari calls this transformation a self-love revolution, and she leads you through it with a devotion and tenacity that makes you excited to do the work.

– Kara McDuffee *MyQuestionLife.com*

Viva the Revolution! Mari's third Journaling Power book is like hopping on a high speed rail ride! She is a stern and compassionate engineer taking you through all of the stops to build the self love that makes the rails to any route to success. *Mindset Medicine* expands on the final chapter of her second Journaling Power book and teaches you how to use your journal to gain the self love, respect and compassion you need to get all of the things you want in your life, all done with Mari's signature storytelling and humor.

– Stephen Van Vugt, Avid Journaler,
www.madmanwithajournal.com

This book is kick-ass! I enjoyed it so much that I highlighted most of it to refer back to later. The journaling prompts are incredible, a favorite was 'write down what you would say to your 10-year-old self as a parent' on page 151. That was good stuff!

– Wendy Kipfmiller-O'Brien, *snixysnix.com*

If you're feeling pressured by societal expectations of what you "should" do, *Mindset Medicine* by Mari L. McCarthy will help deprogram those negative beliefs and allow you to connect with your true authentic self. Through empowering journaling exercises that encourage unconditional self-love, you'll discover your passions and uncover what's been holding you back. I love the idea of marrying yourself! Grab a pen and paper and prepare to get sweet on yourself, realize your life's purpose, and share your gifts with the world!

– Angela Mackintosh, editor-in-chief,
WOW! Women on Writing

Mindset Medicine is a healthy dose of positivity and can-do journaling tips to apply to your life this very minute. Written in a conversational and engaging style, this book is the remedy to the overwhelming overflow of online information and a roadmap to renewal, restoration, and unconditional self-love. Be sure to keep *Mindset Medicine* handy for a booster of confidence and cheer."

– Melanie Faith, Author of *In a Flash!*, *Poetry Power*,
and *Photography for Writers* (*melaniedfaith.com*)

"In *Mindset Medicine*, Mari L. McCarthy champions the idea that appropriate self-love is necessary to live an authentic, empowered life. Using journaling as a tool for healing, she offers warm, supportive guidance to any reader on a path of self-discovery."

– Dennis Palumbo, Psychotherapist and Author,
Writing From The Inside Out

Mindset Medicine

A Journaling Power Self-Love Book

Mari L. McCarthy

Mindset Medicine
A Journaling Power Self-Love book
by Mari L. McCarthy

Published by
Mari L. McCarthy
Mari@CreateWriteNOW.com

ISBN: 978-1098396930 (Print)
LCCN:

Cover and Book Design: Nick Zelinger, NZGraphics.com

First Edition

Printed in the United States of America

To Multiple Sclerosis (MS) for its guidance
and adult supervision in my discovery of
Journaling For The Health Of It®
and ... My True Self!

*"Whatever the mind of man can conceive and believe,
it can achieve."*
—Napoleon Hill

"If you can envision it, you can experience it."
—Mari L. McCarthy

Contents

Introduction

Time to Do Your Self-Love Inner Work

If you've slowly developed a feeling that big tech, mass media, and our cultural and government institutions are doing everything they can to brainwash you, you should pay attention to this feeling.

You should pay attention to it and trust it, because it's your intuition feeding you the truth.

Make no doubt about it, your heart and soul are under siege by societal forces that don't have your best interests in mind. It would be bad enough to say these forces want to separate you from your money, or separate you from your freedom and your privacy. But it's worse than that.

These forces want to separate you from YOU. However, the good news is you have a choice. You can give into these forces and allow them to manipulate you. Or you can join the journaling power revolution, reconnect with your higher self, love yourself unconditionally, and be free to be who YOU really are.

I want you to view this book as an invitation to journey inward and deprogram what you've been conditioned to believe you *should* be. If you're anything like me or most of the people I know, there is so much power within you that has yet to be fully tapped.

This power may be in the form of talents that have gone undiscovered. Desires and passions that have yet to be acted on, or a purpose that hasn't yet been fulfilled.

What I want you to know right now is that every dream, gift, or talent you have is amplified in a big way when you love yourself unconditionally.

You are capable of amazing things. But it can be difficult to be the best version of you when our culture constantly hammers you with messages about what you should be and how you should think.

On the other hand, you receive far fewer messages about how to focus your thoughts, energy, and actions in ways that empower you to feel greater self-love and true inner fulfillment. Instead, you're bombarded by ads, Tweets, and posts that implore you to shut off your brain and follow the herd.

I may not know you personally, but if you've picked up this book and you're reading it, something tells me you have no interest in following the herd or being a cog in a machine. Instead, something tells me you want to nurture your soul, love yourself unconditionally, and be your true authentic self.

If this is what you desire, keep reading because you're in for a fun and fantastic journey. You'll discover how to tap into the power of journaling so you can literally rewire your brain, connect with the true YOU, and love yourself more! I'll reveal how journaling can inspire an energizing change in your consciousness and empower you to make a wondrous shift in your life.

Think of this book as the ultimate lifestyle guide for evolving who you really are at your mental, physical, and spiritual levels. The beauty is you're going to see exactly how you can do this <u>without</u> doctors or prescriptions. If you're willing to step up and do some creative inner work, you'll find out how to form an unbreakable bond with your soul and your true self.

I intend to give you a blueprint to follow that will help you release useless beliefs that are holding you back. As you release them, you'll gain the power to form new ones that allow your light to shine its brightest.

You may discover hidden talents you never knew you had. You may come to a realization that it's okay to throw away useless "stuff" and live a more minimalist lifestyle that's based on self-love and respect. If feelings like this resonate with you, you'll feel empowered to honor them despite the constant messages telling you to buy new things so you can keep up with the latest fashion and technology trends.

You may also find that you can live an infinitely happier life by choosing to tune out the hate and fear that's fed to you on "trash-for-your brain" TV news shows. You may even find you'll just want to throw your TV out the window and be done with it.

If you're tired of being manipulated by an establishment mindset that desperately wants to dictate what you should value, you'll love this book. You'll love it because you'll discover how to cleanse your mind, love yourself more, and set yourself free.

However, doing this isn't going to be some presto-chango magic trick. It won't be as simple as going inward for 20 minutes and then subjecting yourself to the usual noise for the other 23 hours and 40 minutes of your day.

Instead, you and I are going to dig deep and do the work necessary to put YOU back in charge of your life. You'll discover that journaling is a powerful tool that helps you realize what you really want and need in your life. You'll find out where you're stuck and what you need to do to get unstuck.

For example, if deep down inside you have a mission you want to live but haven't, the journaling exercises I'm going to give you will identify this mission.

If, on the other hand, you enjoy seeing yourself as an oppressed victim who is limited in what you can accomplish, your journaling exercises will bring you face to face with this belief.

We're going to uncover everything—warts and all. And when you complete this journey, your "self-love tank" will be spilling over the top.

Bottom line: you and I are about to go on a journey together to a new destination. This destination is a new YOU that is free to achieve anything you want without apology to anyone. Remember, if you can envision it for yourself, you can experience it.

You'll also learn about my story in greater detail. I'll reveal how journaling mitigated many of the physical challenges I faced as a result of having been diagnosed with multiple sclerosis more than 30 years ago.

I'll share with you how, through therapeutic journaling, I was able to ditch my prescription drug routine forever. This empowered me to live the life of my dreams and make an impact in the world far beyond what I did as a Fortune 100 business consultant.

When my first book, *Journaling Power*, became an international bestseller, thousands of people began to share with me their personal stories about how journaling transformed their lives and opened them up to a universe of limitless possibilities.

These wonderful stories from fellow members of the journaling power revolution formed the heart and soul of my second book, *Heal Yourself with Journaling Power*. I concluded the book with a brief chapter on the importance of journaling to create a strong sense of self-love within YOU. As I finished writing the chapter I knew I had much more to say about journaling and self-love. It was at that moment that *Mindset Medicine: A Journaling Power Self-Love Book* was born.

So grant yourself permission to go on a journaling power journey in which you shower yourself with endless amounts of self-love. If you do, I promise it will be the most glorious journey you've ever taken.

You won't need a plane ticket and you won't need to pack a thing. All you'll need is a pen and a pad or a notebook.

I've written *Mindset Medicine* in a style that is simple and straightforward. Each chapter is brief and to the point. Within each chapter, I include a lesson and a journaling prompt. I've made this book very succinct so it's vision is easy to digest and to put into action.

If you want to live a satisfying and fulfilling life, loving the heck out of yourself is a must. In fact, the most powerful thing you can do is to love yourself. If you already do, *Mindset Medicine* will take it to a higher level.

Self-love is at the heart of everything I've written about in my first two books, and now it's the sole focus of *Mindset Medicine.*

Love yourself a lot. It's free, and it's simple to do. There are no contracts or memberships to buy, and you can work at it every day in your journal without breaking a sweat.

I want every page of this book to lead you through a wonderful journey of self-discovery and appreciation for how unique and wonderful you are.

Remember, when you love yourself without conditions, everything you desire will be right at your fingertips.

Let this life-changing journey begin now!

—**Mari L. McCarthy**

Chapter 1

The View from 10,000 Feet

What you and I have in common is that our minds are under continual assault by mental trash that is flying at us from every direction imaginable. If you watch TV, you're receiving repetitive advertising messages about what you should wear, what you should eat, and what you should value. You've got a lot of establishment "shoulds" flying at you.

If you watch cable news at night, you're being told what to believe, what not to believe, who you should love, and who you should hate. You're also being pushed and pulled by people who want you to join their team and despise anyone who sees the world differently. So if you watch cable "news" at night, you've got a lot of hate flying at you.

As these messages are competing for control of your mind, you're also being bombarded by texts, emails, and other intrusive alerts from your phone, tablet, or some other gadget society has decided you must own.

If you get online and look at a website for a few minutes, you can be assured the next time you log into Facebook an ad for that website will be staring you in the face. If this makes you feel as if you're being digitally stalked and hunted, it's because you are. If this makes you feel as if powerful forces are competing to gain control of your mind, it's because they are.

Should you be frightened by all of this? I am not going to say you should. Maybe it scares you or maybe it just makes you feel fed up and angry. That's up to you. However, you should be aware that you're not alone in the feeling that you're being hounded by a never-ending stream of digital madness.

The maximum impact of all this is that it can lessen the love you feel for yourself. At a minimum, it adds up to a bunch of mental noise that you'd prefer to tune out or at least minimize.

I'll get straight to the point. I've written *Mindset Medicine* with the intention of giving you a simple but powerful tool that will help you turn off the noise so you can better control your mental environment and tune into YOU! This tool is unconditional self-love.

Mindset Medicine is also an invitation to join a revolution. If you've ever wanted to put on a bandanna, put a knife between your teeth, and be part of a revolution, this is your chance to join one that's unstoppable. If you don't like guns, don't worry. You won't have to carry one. Instead, your revolutionary weapon of choice is pen-to-paper therapeutic journaling.

So, what is our band of global revolutionaries revolting against? We're revolting against the "should do" mental trash being shoved on us that is dulling our sense of self.

We're revolting against the notion that we're supposed to be brain-dead zombies who follow the herd and do as we're told. We're revolting against the crazy idea that only the top 10% of any demographic have 90% of the wealth, power, and influence of that demographic.

In a nutshell, we're revolting against anything or anyone that would have us believe we should be denied the freedom, opportunity, and power to create the life of our dreams and manifest everything we desire.

Again, our weapon of choice is pen-to-paper journaling. Our intention is to use this weapon to set ourselves free from establishment expectations and get in touch with our inner core, our purpose, and our sense of self-love.

So if you're ready to deal with issues in your tissues and take total command over your destiny—I urge you to take a big bold step right now and join this revolution.

Are you with me?

Good. Welcome aboard. Let's do this!

Your Mindset Medicine Is Right at Your Fingertips

You're well aware that your fingertips give you the ability to pick up prescription pills and pop them in your mouth. But what if you knew they could be used for something more healthy, healing, and liberating? Well they can. In fact, your fingertips can be used to tap into a powerful form of medicine for your mind that is proven to help you:

- Reduce stress and physical pain.
- Overcome illness and other life challenges.
- Heal emotional wounds from past traumas.
- Resolve inner conflicts and improve relationships.
- Gain a deeper understanding of your true authentic self.
- Conquer limiting beliefs and fears that have held you back.

This powerful form of mindset medicine is pen-to-paper therapeutic journaling. The beauty of journaling is that it brings you back to your core, your center, and your soul.

The road to self-love, ongoing peace, and inner serenity really can be paved with a pen. Scientific evidence supports the belief that therapeutic journaling is a transformative tool that empowers you to:

- Discard mental baggage and erroneous thoughts that hold you back.
- Elevate your mood and reduce depression.
- Enjoy the present moment and forgive yourself for past mistakes.
- Unlock powers, talents, and abilities you've previously blocked.
- Set realistic goals and take inspired actions to make them happen.

Studies also indicate that personal traumas, such as bereavement, divorce, or losing your job, can be eased and mitigated through journaling.

The releasing of emotions and pent-up feelings that come through expressive writing is therapeutic for the soul and has a magnificent healing effect on the mind and body.

Journaling brings you back to center and grounds you. It assures that you make time each day to disconnect from the noise that bombards you everywhere you go, so you can be reflective and connect with your inner wisdom.

Now here's the really good news.

You Can Tap into This Healing Power Right Now Because Anyone Can Journal

If I've heard it once I've heard it a million times: "Mari, I'd love to tap into the healing power of journaling, but I can't write very well." To this I say one thing, "Nonsense!" If you can write a shopping list then you have all the talent you need to transform your mind, body, and soul through the healing power of journaling.

Always remember that the only right way to journal is YOUR way. Just put pen to paper and let your natural voice pour forth as if you're having a conversation with your best friend. It really is that simple.

Worried about using proper grammar? Don't be. I mean, who cares about proper grammar when you're writing in your journal. It's not like you have to turn in what you write to be graded by your English teacher from high school.

Sloppy handwriting? Join the club. As long as *you* can read your journal, you're fine. So relax. Have fun with this, and don't hold back. Just be yourself. Just write! And just write knowing no one except you is going to read your journal. Again, if you have the skills to write a shopping or to-do list, you have all the skills you need to be a journaling revolutionary!

Trust me. There's no need to make healing the issues in your tissues more complicated than it needs to be. Just grab a pad and a pen and do it!

Got Proof

Numerous studies around the world provide evidence to support what I've been shouting from the rooftops for years now: "Journaling power has undeniable life-changing health benefits and can absolutely heal the issues in your tissues!"

Here are a few snippets of published studies in peer-review medical journals that support the premise that putting pen to paper unleashes a healing agent that invigorates every cell in your body.

A 2012 review published in the *British Journal of General Practice* notes…

> *"Writing therapy can potentially help 30% of patients who visit primary care settings."*

A published journal review in *Advances in Psychiatric Treatment* concludes…

> *"For some people expressive writing is extremely helpful and has quickly resolved issues that have been mulled over—sometimes for years—with no resolution."*

Many U.S. studies echo these conclusions, as do the words of the renowned Dr. James Pennebaker who says, "As the number of studies increase, it's become clear that writing is far more powerful than anyone has ever dreamed."

More Proof—My Story

I could tell you more about the benefits of therapeutic journaling, and I could share more "professional evidence" from studies that substantiates what I know to be true.

However, the most convincing proof I have is the reports from thousands of people around the world in my *Journaling Power* tribe who've been gracious enough to share their stories with me. Several of these stories are documented in my second book, *Heal Yourself with Journaling Power.*

For the sake of brevity, I am going to share one story that illustrates clearly the role journaling power plays in mindset medicine. The story I'm going to tell you is mine.

If you're not familiar with my story, it's a doozy. So here it is. In my past professional life, I was a high-energy Fortune 100 business consultant. It's true. I was a competitive corporate animal. In and out of airports, hopscotching through time zones, making deals, and doing what I needed to fuel, expand, and power my consulting firm's bottom line. I was damn good at what I did. I was upwardly mobile, and I was enjoying the trappings of success.

But then real life happened.

In 1998, I lost the feeling and function in the right side of my body. Multiple Sclerosis (MS) took them from me. Naturally, I turned to establishment doctors who robotically steered me toward drug-based protocols for treating MS symptoms. I blindly followed along because I'd been conditioned by "medical experts" to take the drugs I was told to take and not to question my doctors.

However, it didn't take long for me to realize that the doctors I was seeing and all of the prescription drugs they were giving me weren't really helping. In fact, they were making me feel worse. I felt like I was just being jerked along through the big pharma machine. I popped pills and felt like crap, while pharma executives popped champagne corks and got rich. Really rich. That's the system.

Finally, I hit rock bottom and decided I had had enough. At my low point, I got up off the deck and began a long journey on which I made the decision to take total control of my health. It wasn't easy to get started. But I took a first step, and then another, and then another … and I just kept going knowing I wouldn't stop until I found a solution that made Mari feel like MARI AGAIN!

I kept at it and dedicated myself to daily ACTION. I began a journaling practice known as Morning Pages. I never could have anticipated how powerful and effective this process would become. It wasn't easy for me, because I was right handed and I had lost the use of the right side of my body. However, I wasn't going to let that stop me, so I slowly taught myself how to write with my left hand.

As I continued my writing practice, my MS symptoms improved. It was amazing. I knew intuitively that my mind was more powerful than I realized. I understood that somewhere within me was a hidden ability to heal myself. In fact, as I continued to journal about my inner feelings and my determination to heal myself, an amazing thing happened:

I was able to ditch my prescription drugs and mitigate most of my MS symptoms through journaling!

Even more important, I discovered, uncovered, and recovered my True Self and even tapped into talents I never knew I had. Best of all, I developed a compassionate relationship with myself and a serenity that provided me with an inner fulfillment I had been forever seeking.

I knew I had stumbled upon something incredible, and my inner voice told me it was my mission to share this discovery with as many people as possible.

So I started **Create Write Now** to share my methods, expertise, and passion for **Journaling For The Health Of It**® with people across the globe who want to master life's challenges and thrive.

It started as a whisper, then it became a movement, and now it's a full-blown worldwide revolution. And you're part of it! The transformation it's going to bring to your life will amaze you. All I can do to back up this claim is to point out what it's done for me.

I've become an international bestselling author who's written two books, *Journaling Power: How to Create the Happy, Healthy Life You Want to Live,* and *Heal Yourself with Journaling Power.*

I've created multiple eBooks and *Journaling Challenge* programs that have had a life-changing impact on countless people around the world.

Through journaling, I was able to dump my prescription drugs, kick aside "conventional establishment" medical wisdom, and mitigate most of my MS symptoms on my own. Now I teach people throughout the world how to heal, grow, and transform their lives through the holistic power of expressive writing.

I also have the pleasure of living in a gorgeous beachfront home in Boston where I have the freedom, flexibility, and physical ability to indulge in all of my passions.

In fact, if you're in my neighborhood you'll usually find me writing, singing, reading, walking the beach, meditating, practicing photography, cheering on the Pittsburgh Steelers, and raising roses and consciousness!

Before uncovering my true self through journaling power, I never dreamed I could become a singer. Well goodbye to limits! In 2015, I released my **third** album, *Lady With a Song,* and I am currently working on my fourth album, *Well-Written Songs.*

I literally created ALL of this through journaling power. I now live life on MY terms, and I am passionately dedicated to helping you do the exact same thing.

If you're not living life on your terms it's because someone or something is holding you back. It could be as simple as society telling you to be something you don't really want to be. It could be the culture in which you live hammering you with messages about what you *should* do and who you *should* be.

If you're not living the life you really want, chances are there are societal forces manipulating you in subtle or not so subtle ways that you may have come to accept. If this makes you angry inside, you're going to love your journaling prompt for this chapter.

Your Journaling Power Prompt

This chapter has examined mindset medicine from a 10,000 foot view, so I want you to take a high-level approach to your first journaling prompt. You're going to like this prompt because it gives you an opportunity to vent and say what's really on your mind. So grab your pad and pen and get ready to write!

If you're new to this revolution, let me repeat my number one journaling power rule: The only right way to journal is YOUR way. Don't worry about good grammar, spelling, and all the other stuff that was pounded into you as a kid.

Just write from your heart! You've probably heard the expression, "Dance like nobody else is watching." This is similar in that I urge you to "Write like no one else will ever read your journal." Just grab your pen and pad, be authentically YOU, and let your thoughts and feelings flow with reckless abandon!

Let's do it!

For your first journaling prompt: I want you to consider an area of your life where you feel you're being manipulated or jerked around by a societal force you're sick and tired of. For me, it was the constant drumbeat coming from the medical establishment that told me the only effective way to deal with my MS symptoms was to follow the herd and consume large quantities of prescription drugs like "normal" Americans do.

This was the issue I chose to revolt against. What's yours?

Do you feel like you're being scared into submission by the self-righteous hate messages streaming your way each night on trashy political TV shows?

Do you feel overwhelmed by the never-ending chant from big media to keep buying and spending so you don't become a "loser" who is out of step with the latest trends?

Do you feel pressured by society to live in a bigger place and pack it with more stuff when in your heart you'd prefer to live a peaceful, scaled-down simple existence?

Whatever the issue in your tissues is, write it down now. Don't hold back. Just pick an issue that's been on your mind and go for it. Write at least a couple pages. The more the better. But just write! Let your honest thoughts and feelings flow forth. Let your feelings start down in your toes and then flow out with power through your pen!

For now, don't worry what action you're going to take to correct the issue that's bugging you. We'll deal with that together in upcoming journaling prompts. Just use this journaling prompt to become completely self-aware about a cultural "you should do this" message that you're ready to fight back against.

Again, don't hold anything back. Just grab your pen and paper and let it rip. Go for it!

Chapter 2

Discovering Your Gifts

In the United States there is a practice that is as steeped in tradition as baseball, hotdogs, and apple pie. I'm not as familiar with the rest of the world, but I'm sure most cultures have a similar tradition.

It's the one where parents, siblings, friends, and/or the media tell, teach, and condition you to believe that it's in your best interest to do something other than what it is you really want to do with your life.

It's a tradition by which people use a variety of tools to bury and suppress the natural talents and gifts with which you came into this world. The tools that are usually used like a hammer to "celebrate" this tradition are fear, jealousy, and resentment. Fear is the big hammer.

It really is a strange tradition when you think about it. You're born with natural talents and interests that stimulate and excite you. And in many cases, these gifts and talents could be used by you to make a positive impact on the lives of others in your local community and even your GLOBAL community! Yet, other people decide that what you "should" do is suppress and bury these talents so deep within you that you eventually forget they exist.

It's astounding what others will do to suppress your natural gifts and talents. However, this practice remains a tradition in most cultures, albeit a really weird one. In fact it's more than weird. It's tragic.

Right now as you read this, your inner voice is screaming at you if you've been a victim of this wicked tradition. However, here is the good news:

Unlike most tragedies, such as a car crash or a crippling injury, you have within you the absolute power to reverse this tragedy no matter how old you are and no matter where you're at in life.

In this chapter we're going to examine how you've fallen victim to this tragic tradition, and how you can use mindset medicine to discover and awaken the true natural talents and gifts with which you've been blessed.

How Family Buries Your Gift

"You're going to go to college and you're going to be either a doctor or a lawyer." Or, "You're not going to go to college, you're going to join the family business and get to work."

Both of these lines are cliches that we've heard countless times in movies and TV. Perhaps you have friends who've been battered over the head with these lines. Or maybe you've been battered and bruised by them.

If you've been a victim of this kind of attack in your life, it was probably carried out by a family member, most likely a parent. Quite often the family member making this attack believed they had your best interest at heart.

They may have believed at the time that their advice or command was needed to put you on a path that would lead you to being safe, sound, and secure. After all, why would you want to be an artist, writer, or a teacher who makes a very modest income when you could be a lawyer or a corporate go-getter who makes lots of money and lives in a nice house?

Hearing these messages from your parents as a child or young adult can be difficult, especially if you have siblings who've caved into this "advice." When your siblings ditch their dreams to go the "safe and secure" route, there's a good chance they'll badger you to "stop dreaming and think realistically." Why? Because if their dreams didn't come true, they may believe that your dreams shouldn't come true either.

On the other hand, when parents and siblings try to suppress your gifts and your dreams, they may not be doing it from a sense of meanness. They may be doing it because they have a learned belief that it's best to go the safe and steady route in life so you can pay your bills and keep a roof over your head.

However, whether their motives are sincere or sinister, the end result is your dreams, gifts, and special talents get squashed or muted.

How Friends Bury Your Gift

Here's another old cliche: "Misery loves company." What this means is that people who have a crappy attitude like hanging out with other people who have a crappy attitude. Or they like being around people who will sympathize with their crappy attitude or victim mentality.

One expression I like is that "you're the average of the five people you hang out with the most." Though it may be a little cliche, there's a lot of truth in this sentiment. This is why it's important "to pick your friends wisely."

The point here is that if you hang out with people who have a bad attitude or a victim mentality, they're not going to want you to be upbeat and enterprising. If you're overweight and you hang out with friends who struggle with their eating habits and do little about it, they may not want to see you lose 20 pounds while they're making another run to Dairy Queen or McDonalds.

If you hang out with people who've suppressed their gifts and dreams to pursue what they've been conditioned to believe is the safe and secure route in life, they're not going to encourage you to break free and pursue your dreams with gusto and enthusiasm.

Again, misery loves company. Friends and colleagues may not use the same mental sledgehammer to suppress your gifts and talents that parents and siblings do. Instead, they may use a more subtle form of conditioning in the hopes of keeping you as dissatisfied as they are. After all, they like you just the way you are and they may rely on your dissatisfaction with life to validate their own dissatisfaction.

The bottom line here is that hanging out with the wrong people could further bury your talents and gifts deeper within you.

How Establishment Media Noise Buries Your Gifts

When I was younger I had a sense that the media's primary job was to inform you. Today, I have a strong sense that its primary goal is to scare the hell out of you. The news shows push hate and conflict and a belief that life as we know it "will never be the same" if the wrong political team wins.

If that's not enough, advertisers are determined to make you feel like a loser if you're not blindly buying into the latest consumer trends. How can you afford to finance the slickest fashions, the newest cars, and the hottest tech gadgets advertisers tell you to buy? Well, you need to make a lot of money, which may mean setting your dreams aside to find a job that pays you the most money. Sure, you may hate the job—but so what, you need to buy new stuff so you can "keep up."

You're constantly bombarded by messages to buy more, consume more, and apply for the trendy new credit card so you can earn a lot of "points." Seldom do you hear any messages that implore you to get out of debt, cut back on the number of shoes you own, and live a more minimalist lifestyle so you have the freedom to pursue your true talents and passions.

The end result is that it's easy to feel as if you need to spend more, have more, Tweet more, and post more. At the same time, you're supposed to be simultaneously afraid of what might happen with the stock market, the housing market, or the threat you face from people who don't look or think like you.

Keep spending, but be afraid. The anxiety you feel as this mixed media message hammers away at you continually can be another force that pushes your talents and dreams deeper within you.

Why "Should" Is the Dirtiest Word of All

You have to be a certain age to remember legendary comedian George Carlin. Carlin was someone who certainly shared his gift with the world, and he certainly didn't die without making the most of it.

Perhaps his most famous comedy bit was one about the seven dirty words you can never say on television. As you might expect, all seven words were quite "tawdry" to put it mildly. However, as funny as this comedy routine was, George left one word off his list that I believe is the dirtiest word of all.

That word is *should*.

Think of all the times in your life you've been told what you *should* do. Now think about all the time you've wasted racking your brain about what you *should* do when confronted with choices in your personal and professional lives.

If there's one word that's going to single-handedly drive your dreams and talents into an internal ditch deep within you—it's the word *should*.

That's because the word *should* is so debilitating. It forces you into a small box in which you're led to believe you've made a big mistake if you don't do what other people believe you *should* do.

Think of all the times you've been told family, friends, and society that:

- You *should* take a certain job because it's more secure (allegedly).
- You *should* buy the newest phone because it has faster download speeds.
- You *should* buy more useless "stuff" for your home that you'll never use.
- You *should* fall in love with this person instead of that person.
- You *should* eat this way instead of that way.

The word should puts you under a lot of pressure to conform and it can cause you to doubt the wisdom of your inner voice. This is why the word *should* can be so debilitating.

However, what will happen if everytime people and society hammered you with the word *should*, you replaced it with the word *could*? I can tell you from experience exactly what will happen. FREEDOM will happen.

This is because the word *could* isn't debilitating. Instead, the word *could* is liberating.

It's liberating because it gives you choices. Here's your proof. Let's look at the same bulleted list of "should" phrases I shared with you a moment ago. If you replace the word *should* with the word *could* in each bullet point, here's what you get:

- You *could* take a certain job because it's more secure (allegedly).
- You *could* buy the newest phone because it has faster download speeds.
- You *could* buy more useless "stuff" for your home that you'll never use.
- You *could* fall in love with this person instead of that person.
- You *could* eat this way instead of that way.

Notice the difference. The word *could* gives you options and choices. It liberates you because when you replace *should* with *could* your mind automatically asks you this beautifully wonderful question:

"I could do this or that. So, what do I WANT to do?"

When you ask the question, "What do I WANT to do?" your heart begins to speak to you—quite loudly in most cases. When your heart begins to speak to you an amazing thing happens. You find yourself in a position where you get to FEEL your best decisions. This is much more joyful than being in a place where you have to make your best decisions.

This liberation occurs simply by changing the word *should* to *could*. So from this point forward in your life, everytime you're slammed with a message about what you *should* do— throw out the word *should* and replace it with *could*.

Instead of feeling pressured to conform, you'll feel liberated and be in a powerful position to do what you WANT.

The bottom line is this: when you replace the word *should* with *could*, it's much easier to keep your dreams and talents closer to the surface of your soul.

Get Mad as Hell and Make a Pledge Not to Take it Anymore

As you can clearly see, there are many forces that conspire to drive your dreams, talents, and desires so far inside you that you don't see them anymore. But now it's time to fight back and do something about it.

And when I say fight back, I mean fight back! Here's how you're going to start this fight.

One of my favorite iconic movie lines comes from the 1976 film, *Network*. In it, the character Howard Beale stands up at his desk during a newscast and yells with all his might, "I'm as mad as hell and I'm not going to take this anymore!"

He then implores his audience to run to their windows, open them, and scream this message out to the world—which they do. If you haven't seen this legendary scene, it's easy to find on YouTube.

The message Howard Beale imparts from his news desk before his famous outburst is as meaningful today as it was in 1976. If you vaguely remember watching the film *Network* over 40 years ago, this scene is definitely worth watching again.

Howard Beale told his television listeners to open their windows and yell, "I'm as mad as hell and I'm not going to take this anymore!"

I kind of want you to do the same thing. Now, I'm a journaling power revolutionary so I'd implore you to write this down in your journal if you feel so moved. But, if you're in the mood to open your window and let your neighbors know how you feel—then by all means, go for it!

My point is this: now that you know there are forces at work that are trying to keep you from being YOU, it's time to take the action needed to unbury your true talents and gifts and put them at your fingertips.

If you make a pledge to yourself to take this action, your life can be anything you want it to be. In fact, it can be amazing. If you want to know how amazing it can be, just ask yourself a few simple questions.

How will you feel if you make the most of your gifts?

If you know you have talents and gifts that you've buried deep inside you, how much more alive and vibrant will you feel if you tap into them and bring them to the forefront of your life?

Suppose you have an ear for music and have always wanted to play the guitar. But you repressed this talent because you were told that musicians don't make money. So instead, you became a dentist or an engineer because it was drilled into you that this would lead to a life that was "safe and secure."

After all, musicians don't get "benefits packages." Engineers do.

How would you feel if you finally brought your gift for music to the surface of your soul and began to play an instrument? Even if it was just something you did on nights and weekends.

Would you feel more enriched and more fulfilled? Would you love yourself more?

Who will you meet that you otherwise wouldn't?

Let's stick with my musician example for a moment. If you brought your talent for music to the surface and began to play an instrument, who would you meet that you otherwise wouldn't? Well, you'd probably meet other like-minded souls who play instruments and love music. This could create a new set of friends for you and a feeling of comfort that comes when you engage with a community of people who share your passion.

Even if bringing your hidden talents and gifts to the surface doesn't lead to a new career, it can lead to a much greater sense of belonging. This alone makes it worthwhile to tap into your hidden gifts. If doing so leads you to a community where you make just a few new friends, there's no telling how many stepping stones will appear before you that lead down magical paths to fulfilling journeys.

Who is waiting to hear from you?

This is a very exciting question to ask yourself as you go through the process of tapping into your hidden gifts. It's an exciting question because today the world is interconnected like never before through online communities.

When I began my Morning Pages journaling routine over 20 years ago, it was just me, my pen, and my journal. Today it's my pen, my journal, and my amazing global community of journaling power revolutionaries. What a change from when I started!

What I learned as my journaling practice developed is that I could help legions of people who wanted to develop their own journaling practice. Most importantly, I learned that to help others you don't need to be the super-talented guru who sits high atop the mountain. I discovered you only need to be a few steps ahead of those you wish to help pull up the mountain.

So if your hidden talent is speaking about self-development, there are people waiting to hear from you. If you're an average musician, beginning musicians are waiting to hear from you. If you have a passion for fitness training and healthy eating, people who'd like to lose weight and get in better shape are waiting to hear from you.

Again, through today's technology the people waiting to hear from you can be anywhere in the world. With an internet connection and a few mouse clicks, you can reach them and change their lives for the better. All because you made the simple choice to "get mad as hell" and unbury your hidden gifts despite what society and other people said you "should" do.

So, are you ready to finally throw caution to the wind and bring your hidden talents and gifts to the surface of your soul? I hope you are. But if you're not, I have to ask you one more question.

What's Holding You Back?

In this chapter you and I have examined the subtle and direct forces that conspire to bury your gifts and talents so deep within you that they become hidden.

However, you've also become aware of the beautiful new world and inner fulfillment that awaits you if you choose to do the work needed to bring your gifts out into the light.

So if you're still hesitating to take action, what's holding you back is most likely fear. Fear of the unknown, fear of change, fear of disappointing others... the list goes on.

When it's time to do the inner work needed to make changes in your life, it's understandable that you may feel fearful or anxious. However, one way to overcome fear is to remember why you feel fear in the first place.

Fear was hardwired into our DNA a heck of a long time ago as a means of protecting us from physical danger. In most cases, this meant protecting us from wild animals that might be interested in turning us into a meal while we were venturing outside our cave to gather some food.

Our brains are wired to scan for potential danger that could bring us harm. Yet, in modern society we're physically safer now than at any point in human history. In a nutshell, your fear mechanism is intended to save you from being harmed physically. It isn't intended to save you from being your best version of YOU. There isn't any reason to be fearful in your quest to tap into your hidden gifts and talents.

Now, it's understandable that a little fear and all of the crap that's been piled on you for years or decades by friends, family, and the media might make it a challenge to uncover your inner gifts. But now is the time to break free from any anxiety you may feel so you can live a life that is energizing and exhilarating.

Your journaling prompt will help you do this.

Your Journaling Power Prompt

Deep down inside, you know you have a unique ability that could impact the lives of a lot of people in a positive way. Or maybe you have an interest or ability like drawing or painting that you haven't tapped into that would bring you a great deal of pleasure.

You may also have a hidden talent that is aching to make its way to the surface. For me, it was singing. Wayne Dyer was famous for saying, "Don't die with your music still in you," and I'm thankful that I won't. Tapping into my hidden talent for singing has brought a great deal of joy to my life.

Your journaling prompt for this chapter is about identifying the music that's still inside of you. Your "music" could be anything. It could be a talent, like singing, drawing, writing. Maybe you have a talent for engineering or making furniture that's aching to come out. Or perhaps you have a desire to volunteer at an animal shelter or participate in a charitable cause that would bring you inner fulfillment.

Again, your "music" could be anything. Deep down inside, I'm sure you know what it is. And even deeper down inside is a mental barrier that prevents you from bringing this gift to the surface.

In this chapter, we've explored how establishment society, family, and the media can build barriers, create noise, and incite fear that keeps you from pursuing that which you really love.

So, your journaling prompt has three simple parts and an "extra credit" part if you're bold enough to get after it—and I'm sure you are!

First, write a few paragraphs or a page or more about a hidden desire, gift, or talent that is buried within you and screaming to come out. A simple way to start this prompt is to begin by writing this:

"I feel I am making the most of the gifts God (Spirit, Source, Universe) has given me when I am..." From this point, just let your writing flow from your heart. If you do this, whatever is hidden inside you will come out with full force.

Second, write a few paragraphs or more about the barrier that keeps you from bringing your hidden gift to the surface. Have you been hammered by others with messages about what you "should" be doing? Have societal forces instilled a level of fear in you that holds you back? Do you have an internal belief dating back to your childhood that's suppressing this gift?

Whatever it is, write it down. Get clear on your gift, and get clear about what's been stopping you from tapping into it.

Third, write a few paragraphs or more about what you're absolutely committed to doing to break through the barrier that stands between you and making the most of your hidden gift. This could be anything. Maybe you need to change jobs. Or maybe you just need to change or adjust one hour in your daily routine.

Whether the change you need to make is big and bold or soft and subtle, commit to it with your journaling power revolutionary spirit. Also, remember to love yourself through this process. Perhaps the change you need to make can be accomplished in a day or a week. On the other hand, it may require a series of baby steps that you execute over a year or more. Be determined with this part of your journaling prompt, but be good to yourself and avoid burdening your mind with undue stress.

The key here is to write down what effective action you're committed to taking to break down the barrier that prevents you from squeezing all of the joyful juice you can from a gift or talent you know you have.

Do you want to earn a little extra credit? Are you bold enough to take on this extra step? I think you are, because you're a journaling power revolutionary. So here it is.

Picture your life one, three, five, or 10 years from now. Then, write a few paragraphs or more about how your life will look and feel if you DON'T make the effort to break through your barrier and fully leverage your hidden talent or desire.

You can start by simply asking yourself this question: "How will the end of my life feel if I *do* allow myself to die with my music still inside of me?"

This is a tough question and answering it honestly will not make you happy. In fact, it will probably make you feel a little down in the dumps. It could be the spark that motivates you to identify the music buried within you. And it could be the spark that compels you to tap into your hidden gift, desire, or talent and share it with the world.

There you go. This journaling prompt is simple, but it has a lot of meat on the bone. Grab your pen and pad, ignite your revolutionary spirit, and get after it!

Chapter 3

You Have to Love Yourself First

Once you've unburried your hidden gifts and brought them to the surface, the way to make the most of them is to leverage the most powerful form of mindset medicine—unconditional self-love.

Those who possess a deep sense of self-love live fulfilling and satisfying lives. Those who are unable to love themselves live tortured lives. This sounds tough, but it's true.

The good news is that self-love is a choice. This means you have the power to make it infinitely easier to live a fulfilling and glorious life.

So choose to shower yourself with endless love every day of your life. Marry yourself, worship yourself, and be forever grateful for how wonderful you are.

Consider this important point:

If you don't love yourself, who will? If you don't love yourself, how can you expect anyone else to love you as much as you want to be loved?

You don't have to be arrogant about it, but it is 100% perfectly fine to be in love with yourself. In fact, it's extremely essential to be in love with yourself. When you love yourself, you make it much easier for other people to love you too.

Think about it. What have you got to lose by loving yourself? Absolutely nothing.

What have you got to lose by not loving yourself? Absolutely everything.

It's kind of a no-brainer, isn't it. So cut yourself some slack and muster up all the self-love you can.

The first step in doing this is to cast aside negative notions about self-love that have been fed to you by society for decades.

Here's an example.

How many times in your life have you heard someone (maybe even you?) say something like this: "That guy is a jerk, he's so in love with himself!"

I think we've all said this about someone. Adding to our frustration with people we've labeled as "being in love with themselves" is the recognition that so many of them seem to always get what they want, and they always seem to be happy about it.

The nerve of these people!

However, instead of criticizing people who are in love with themselves, maybe you could instead model their behaviors and beliefs.

Loving yourself is the healthiest thing you can do.

If everyone was passionately in love with themselves, do you think it would have a negative or positive effect on your home, your community, your state, and your country?

It's accepted universally that society would be much more pleasant and productive if we all loved each other. So it stands to reason that things would be even BETTER if we all loved ourselves.

Have you ever wanted to be a leader in your community? Here's your chance. Join the unconditional—self-love revolution, step out front, and lead the way!

The world will be a better place because of it.

The world will be a better place because unconditional self-love is the greatest gift you can give yourself. It's the greatest gift you can give yourself because self-love is the key to getting and staying embodied.

This is essential given you are probably very experienced at letting your head overwhelm you with things to worry about. In our frenzied e-sludge society, we've become experts at overanalyzing our lives and finding things to keep us up at night when we should be sleeping.

Isn't it amazing that you're told constantly through the media that to get a good night's sleep you need better pillows, expensive mattresses, and the finest sheets in all the land.

In short, society tells you that to get a good night's sleep you need to spend a lot of money on better sleeping equipment. That's nuts!

The truth is, to get a better night's sleep all you have to do is to love yourself more. Imagine how much easier it would be to get a good night's rest if when your head hits the pillow you are thinking blissfully about how much you love and adore YOU.

Do you want to make each and every day as productive as it could be? Then sleep well every night. If you want to sleep well every night, love yourself more.

Feel Fully Embodied

Unconditional self-love is nature's sleeping pill, and it is also nature's "gateway drug" to feeling fully embodied and connected to your divine self.

Loving yourself puts you at peace and makes you feel at home in your body. In a deeper sense, self-love enables you to be more present, more connected to Spirit *(Spirit, God, Him, Her...you pick the word that works for you)*, and to feel every wonderful sensation in your body.

When you love yourself, you feel as though you have a safe and healthy way to express your needs, desires, wants, fears, and doubts. You're able to self-soothe your soul when you feel agitated or frustrated.

An authentic sense of self-love connects you to every aspect of your heart and soul so you can identify your innermost needs and attend to them with care. You also gain an intuitive ability to recognize and correct cognitive imbalances that may be zapping your energy and limiting your productivity.

Put simply: self-love is the secret sauce of life and you deserve to bathe in it!

There's more good news.

There is a process for creating a grand sense of unconditional self-love within YOU. This process is revealed in this book and I am confident you will master it.

You'll master it by taking baby steps and creating unstoppable momentum as you move through the lessons and journaling prompts within each chapter. I encourage you to refer back to these lessons and prompts as often as you need to.

My mission is to make this journey joyful and comforting. As you read each word of this book, I ask that you agree to be good to yourself and see every moment of this journey as a refuge in which you feel safe, secure, and loved.

Your Journaling Power Prompt

In this chapter I am going to give you a very simple journaling prompt, but it may be one of the more challenging things you've done.

Here it is.

Grab your pen and write "I love myself" in your journal.

In addition, I want you to think about the last time you wrote this simple little sentence about yourself. I also want you to be honest and admit if you've never written this before!

Next, I want you to write, "I love myself" again. Then write it several more times.

This won't take long. It's only three words. Three incredibly wonderful and powerful words that will transform your life.

Now, I want you to get bold.

I want you to say "I love myself" OUT LOUD several times.

And when I say out loud, I don't mean just move your lips a little as you mumble to yourself.

I mean, say "I LOVE MYSELF" out loud. Really out loud. Not once, not twice, but several times.

Say it with a big sloppy grin across your face. This will make you feel amazing because it's very difficult, if not impossible, to put a big smile on your face and feel lousy.

For the next step in this journaling prompt, and this is the big part, I want you to take your journal and stand in front of a mirror. Come on, do it!

I want you to stand in front of a mirror, put a big smile on your face, look yourself square in the eyes, and say, "I love myself." Not once, not twice, but several times.

Now I know you may be thinking, "I'm with you on this, Mari, but do I really have to look at myself in the mirror and say 'I love you' to myself out loud?"

Yes, you do!

I am going to explain why by asking you two questions:

How many times have you written about how much you love yourself?

How many times have you stood in front of your mirror and talked about how much you love yourself?

I'm guessing you probably haven't done these two things in a long time, if ever.

On the other hand, I bet there have been numerous times over the years when you have stood in front of your mirror and said things like:

"What the hell's wrong with you?"
"Why'd you do that?"
"How come you're not in better shape?"
Why don't you have more money?
"Why don't you try harder."
"You're worthless."
"You talk too much."

If you've done this, you're certainly not alone. We have all abused ourselves while looking in the mirror for one reason or another.

But how many times have you stood in front of your mirror and said:

"I love you! You're dreamy and incredible!"

If you're not doing this every single day of your life, my next question is:

Why the heck not?!

It certainly doesn't take long.

If you're not doing this simple little exercise every day, you're not doing it enough. But now you can make up for it.

Shower yourself with self-love. Do this every day. Write down the words, "I love you" in your journal. Then stand in front of your mirror and say, "I love you" to yourself.

Remember to say it loud and say it proud.

After the ass kicking you've been giving yourself in front of your mirror for all of these years, it's time to turn the tables and get the self-love thing going.

Getting good at smothering yourself with love can be your own private little thing.

No one even has to know you're doing it. You can love yourself while you're writing in your journal every day and no one will suspect a thing.

When you give yourself permission to finally love yourself, it will put you in a tremendous frame of mind for attracting what you really want in all areas of your life.

So go for it. You have nothing to lose and endless amounts of joy to gain.

Let's keep it rolling. You're going to get good at this!

Chapter 4

You Are Worthy and Deserve Everything You WANT

There are endless reasons to envelop yourself in a continuous state of unconditional self-love. Perhaps the greatest reason is that self-love fuels your self-esteem and gives you a positive sense of self-worth, which is critical to your belief system.

If you don't have a positive sense of self-worth you will develop a belief system that says you don't deserve *this*, or you're not worthy of *that*. If this negative pattern continues throughout your life it can have devastating consequences.

Feelings that you're not worthy or deserving of something can mean being poor instead of enjoying financial abundance. It can mean feeling down and lethargic instead of positive and energized. It can also mean living alone and being isolated instead of sharing your life with someone you love deeply.

Not feeling worthy or deserving can completely change your life for the worse, because we tend to associate these feelings with areas of our lives that are of massive importance. For example, you probably have never found yourself in a state in which you internalized beliefs such as, "I don't feel worthy of going on a walk in the park today," or "I'm not good enough to watch this TV show tonight."

On the other hand, you may have found yourself struggling with "big-ticket" thoughts, such as:

- "I don't deserve to be wealthy, because I'm not smart enough to get rich."
- "I'm not worthy of meeting my true soulmate. I'll just have to settle for what I can get."
- "I struggle with my willpower, so I don't deserve to be fit and trim."

I see beliefs as simply thoughts that you think over and over again. When you have negative beliefs, you put out negative vibrations. When you put out negative vibrations, you're not going to attract great things into your life.

This is why it is so crucial to work on the beliefs you have about being worthy and deserving of wonderful things when it comes to your wealth, health, and relationships.

What is typically the root cause of feeling that you're not worthy or deserving of something? The answer is simple.

Feeling you don't deserve *this* or you're not worthy of *that* stems from a lack of self-love. Worse yet, not loving yourself begins a terrible cascade effect in your life, because if you don't love yourself, you will develop a negative belief system.

When you develop a negative belief system, you put out negative vibrations. Again, when you put out negative vibrations, you attract negative things into your life. When you develop limiting beliefs, you put limits on what you can attract.

So, if you believe you do not deserve to be rich—you're not going to attract wealth into your life.

If you believe you're not worthy of meeting your soulmate —you will have to settle for less.

If you believe you can't lose weight and get trim and fit - good luck losing weight.

Apply this pattern to other areas of your life and you can see how devastating the consequences can be over the course of your lifetime.

When you have feelings of being unworthy or undeserving, it creates resistance within your mind, body, and soul, which cuts you off from the universal flow of good things that desperately want to come your way.

However, there is a really simple way to avoid such resistance and manifest all that you desire.

The Magic of Self-Love

Unconditional self-love is the mindset medicine that empowers you to ditch any feelings you have about being worthy of this or that.

This is because when you love yourself without conditions, you find it very easy simply to give yourself permission to WANT things like abundant wealth, exceptional health, and fantastic relationships.

When you love yourself, it's easy to put a big grin on your face and say you WANT something. The joy of WANTING something can easily become your dominant vibration and override any deep-rooted thoughts about whether or not you deserve it.

When you love yourself deeply, it's easy to put yourself in a joyous state in which you think energizing and liberating thoughts, such as :

- "Who cares if I'm not 'worthy' of being rich—
  I WANT to create great wealth anyway!"

- "I'm not concerned with whether I 'deserve' to find my soulmate—I WANT to meet my soulmate and I won't settle for less until I do."
- "So what if I'm not 'worthy' of being a fitness model because of my age and genetics, I WANT to be in the best possible shape I can be, so I'm going to make it happen."

Remember, it's ok to WANT things. WANTING great things for yourself doesn't make you selfish. WANTING great things for YOU just means you love yourself.

So go ahead and WANT great health, financial abundance, and incredible relationships. Spend the rest of today simply WANTING things and discover how great it feels.

When you love yourself and want things, thoughts about being worthy or deserving of them will melt away and be forgotten. This will completely change the vibration you put out to the Universe.

Self-Love + WANTING = Excitement

Remember the joy of wanting that came naturally to you as a child? Remember how wonderful that made you feel, especially around the holidays.

When you were 10 years old and you WANTED a particular new toy, did you spend any time thinking about whether you were worthy of it or whether you deserved it? Probably not.

You just WANTED that toy, and the feeling filled you with excitement and anticipation of receiving it ... somehow, some way.

You didn't question your worthiness when you were a child, you just wanted things. Well, why not do the same thing now?

Love yourself and WANT things! Again, it's not selfish to want. In fact, one of the things you can want is the means to help more people. All the more reason to want financial abundance.

Plus, wanting creates a feeling of joy, anticipation, and excitement in your life. And the excitement of wanting creates a powerful vibration that attracts like a magnet.

So, drop your feelings of being unworthy and undeserving, and replace them with the excitement of sheer UNAPOLO-GETIC WANTING!

This will put you in a tremendous vibrational state in which you are more open to receiving everything you desire.

Again, when you give yourself permission simply to WANT something, feelings of being unworthy or undeserving of it will simply melt away.

Your Journaling Power Prompt

Put yourself in a child-like state and make this journaling prompt a lot of FUN. This is a simple three-step prompt, and I really want you to go bananas with it!

Step 1

Again, put yourself in a child-like mindset and start dreaming of all the things you WANT in your life. Don't hold anything back! Just go for it! Pretend you're a kid again and list all the toys and gifts you want to receive in your life.

Dream big, and just start writing. Put a big sloppy grin on your face and don't leave out a thing. Have fun with this!

Want a new car? Write it down. Want a new wardrobe? Write it down. Want to meet the lover of your dreams? Write it down. Want to be in the best physical and emotional shape of your life? Write it down.

Don't stop until you have a complete list of everything you WANT!

Step 2

Go back through your list and write a few sentences about why you want each item. Again, don't hold anything back. Spread a joyous grin across your face and put yourself in a child-like state.

Write with abandon and shower yourself with love. Have fun and don't for one second entertain any silly ideas about whether you deserve what you want. Just have a good time and write why you want what you want.

Remember, it's perfectly healthy to just WANT things. The more you have, the more you can give to others!

Step 3

Now that you've written a list of things you absolutely want for yourself, and you've included a fun-filled explanation detailing why you want them, I want you to do one final thing.

For every item on your list, write down how wonderful it's going to make you feel when it arrives in your life. Again, be joyous and don't hold anything back!

Remember how you would lie awake at night when you were a kid, dreaming about how great life was going to be when you received the gift you had your heart set on getting for your birthday? Remember the excitement and anticipation that spread through your soul?

Do the exact same thing with your list. Write down how glorious it's going to make you feel as you receive each item on your list that you want ...for no other reason other than you really WANT it.

When you do this journaling prompt (all three steps!), you'll discover how healthy and natural it feels simply to want things.

Remember, if you receive everything you want you are in a much stronger position to help other people.

When you truly give yourself permission to love yourself and rediscover the joyous feeling of WANTING something, useless notions about whether you're worthy of it will drift away forever.

Chapter 5

Declare Why Others Must
Respect YOU

As you've now discovered, unconditional self-love is the key to giving yourself permission to WANT anything you desire. When you love yourself without conditions, you free yourself from a negative belief system that has you questioning whether you're *worthy* or *deserving* of what you want.

Yet, there's much more that unconditional self-love can ignite within you, so let's keep the momentum rolling!

When you shower yourself with unconditional self-love it is infinitely easier to infuse your being with a tremendous sense of self-respect.

Throughout your life, you've heard how important it is to respect yourself. However, without unconditional self-love as your foundation, it's difficult to maintain a strong sense of self-respect.

If you don't feel unconditional love for yourself, self-respect can only be achieved through sheer determination. Unfortunately, sheer determination requires a lot of energy. And when you rely on determination to feel respect for yourself, the feeling will ebb and flow and come and go.

Using determination to create self-respect is similar to using will power to control your weight. Sometimes you have a lot of willpower, but sometimes you don't. This is why people who use willpower to control their eating tend to lose weight, then gain it back, then lose a little, and then gain even more back.

The end result is a cycle of frustration that leads to burnout and a sense of failure. A similar cycle occurs when you rely on determination to create self-respect.

The bottom line is this: you cannot develop and maintain a strong sense of self-respect through affirmations and determination. You can only develop a lasting and ever-flowing sense of self-respect when you feel unconditional love for yourself.

Only with unfettered self-respect can you face the world and be YOU in an unapologetic way!

Reverse Your Thinking—Change Your Life

When the foundation of your life is unconditional self-love, self-respect runs on autopilot. No longer will feeling respect for yourself require determination. Instead, it will flow with effortless ease.

This tidal change within your central nervous system will reverse your thinking in ways that will change your life dramatically.

When self-love and self-respect flow naturally through your being, you praise yourself and no longer beat up on yourself. Mistakes go from being viewed as failures to being seen as learning opportunities.

You no longer wallow in stress in any given situation as you think about what you *should* do. Instead, you relax and consider the different things you *could* do. As you bask in the freedom of thinking about what you could do, you ultimately feel the joy and satisfaction of deciding what you WANT to do.

This emotional freedom only comes when you bathe yourself in the light and breezy vibration that comes through unconditional self-love and self-respect. When this glorious feeling is your natural "default" state, you no longer tolerate disrespect from others. Instead, you not only expect others to respect you—you insist on it.

Ask and Require More!

Are there areas of your life where you could be demanding more respect from others? If so, what's stopping you from putting your foot down and requiring it?

The key word here is *require*. Demanding respect conjures up images of people who are upset, raising their voice, and venting frustration over the fact they're not receiving the level of respect they desire.

Demanding respect isn't good enough. Why? Because demanding something is typically just a loud way of *asking* for it.

When you truly love yourself without condition, it is infinitely easier to stay calm and cool and require others to respect you in every situation.

When you demand something, sometimes you'll get it and sometimes you won't. However, when you require something, you emanate a vibration that says, "Either I get it or I'm out of here."

Show me a person who is able to stay calm, cool, and collected and require that he or she be respected, and I'll show you someone who has an unwavering sense of self-love.

Ask yourself if you're receiving the level of respect from others that you want in every area of your life.

Is your spouse or significant other giving you the respect you desire? How about clients or co-workers? Do your children show you the respect you deserve? What about your friends and others in your social network and community? Are they showing you the level of respect you require?

If the answer to any of these questions is "no," you have to ask yourself why this is. Could it have anything to do with the level of self-love you have for yourself?

I bet it does.

With this in mind, ask yourself what it will take for you to REQUIRE more respect from people in every area of your life. I'm certain when you think this through you'll realize that to require more respect from others, you must first increase the level of love you feel for yourself.

In the end, the level of respect you require from others is tied directly to the level of love and respect you have for yourself. So raise it!

Imagine How Your Life Will Look

How will you feel and how will you present yourself to the world if you require an optimum level of respect from everyone in your life? How will you walk? How will you talk? How will you breathe? How much more certain will you feel?

How will requiring an optimum level of respect from others affect your health, your wealth, and your relationships? When you answer these questions, think about the answers you'd give if you were looking at your life today, a year from now, three years from now, and five years from now.

Think about the massive impact on your life if you simply require an optimum level of respect from everyone you know! Consider the amazing power you will feel as you continue to love and respect yourself more each day.

People who love and respect themselves put out a bright light and an aura that we often call *charisma*. We are all attracted to charismatic people. We admire them because charismatic people are charming, engaging, and certain.

The underlying foundation of people who exhibit these character traits is self-love and self-respect. This is why people we see as charismatic tend to attract that which they desire like a magnet.

This is an incredible power to possess, and the ability to create it is right at your fingertips. So grab your pen and pad right now!

Your Journaling Power Prompt

Write down five areas of your life where you are not showing yourself enough self-respect. Be honest with yourself. Focus your thoughts right now on key areas of your life, such as your health, your profession, and your relationships. Be as specific as you can, and write like no one but you will ever see what you're putting down on paper.

Next, write down how each of these five areas of your life can look vastly different if you merely love yourself more and show yourself a higher level of respect. Consider how your life will look a year from now, three years from now, and five years now if you do this.

Next, write about how your life may look five years from now if you *don't* love and respect yourself more.

Lastly, write a strong, certain, and definitive statement about why you are 100% committed to REQUIRING more respect from others. Make unconditional self-love and self-respect the backbone of this statement.

Be confident, assert yourself, and be YOU!

Chapter 6

Establish Rock-Solid Boundaries

By this point in your journey, you should be building some serious self-love momentum, and it should be pretty clear that self-love is like a magic potion that can transform your life in incredible ways. To further build this momentum in chapter six, I'm first going to repeat two key points from chapter five:

> When you truly love yourself without condition, it is infinitely easier to require others to respect you in every situation.

> In the end, the level of respect you require from others is tied directly to the level of love and respect you have for yourself.

When you love yourself and require respect from others, it is significantly easier to establish definite boundaries in your life. This is the point I really want to drive home in this chapter. You simply cannot live a full, satisfying life and truly be YOU in the world unless you have the confidence to set clear-cut boundaries that you never allow others to violate.

Establishing firm boundaries with people is incredibly vital to living a happy and joyous life. It is also much, much easier to do this when you love and respect yourself without conditions.

When you don't have firm boundaries in your life, other people will sense this and take advantage of you or push you into directions you don't want to go.

Has this ever happened to you? I'm sure it has. I know it has certainly happened to me. The sad fact is, people tend to push around or trample over other people they sense are weaker than they are. People never try to push around people who are stronger than they are.

This "rule of the jungle" certainly applies to physical strength. However, that's not what I'm talking about here, because we very rarely find ourselves (*although it does happen occasionally*) in situations where someone is trying to violate our boundaries physically.

On the other hand, I'm sure you have to deal with situations daily where people challenge your emotional, spiritual, and psychological boundaries. These are the boundaries I want you to strengthen and fortify. A great way to do this of course is through journaling power!

Let's look at some areas in your life where feeling unconditional self-love and self-respect will empower you fully to establish boundaries that cannot be penetrated.

Professional Boundaries

Setting boundaries in your professional life can be very challenging. This is because if you work for someone else, you probably have a boss who can tell you what to do at any given moment throughout the day.

In today's constantly-connected digital age, it is very difficult to establish professional boundaries if you have an employer who doesn't hesitate to text or email you at 6 a.m., in the evenings, and even right smack dab in the middle of a relaxing Sunday afternoon.

If you run your own business, you probably have customers and/or clients who feel they can boss you around and make unreasonable demands of your time. Again, this can come in the form of texts or emails on a Sunday morning. Boundary violators can also be clients who just assume you'll gladly work 20 hours over a weekend to accommodate their deadline demands.

Are you dealing currently with such "boundary violations" in your professional life? If you are, I want you to think about why you continue to put up with them. I also want you to identify what it is that's holding you back from "putting your foot down" and establishing boundaries that cannot be penetrated.

Is it fear? Are you afraid of losing your job or losing a client? Is it a poor self-image? Is it a lack of personal respect or a lack of self-love? Do you feel inferior to the person violating your boundaries?

For now, just think about this. I'll have you attack this issue in your tissue with your pen and paper at the end of this chapter. But for now, just think about it.

Personal Boundaries

Having your personal boundaries violated may not evoke the same fear as having your professional boundaries violated, but personal boundary violations can be equally frustrating and they can certainly waste your time and drain your energy.

On a day-to-day basis, violations of your personal boundaries may be relatively harmless. But again, the time and energy they drain over time can be significant. Or to put it another way, they can slowly suck the life out of you.

What am I talking about here? I'm talking about the nosy "friend" who continually pries into your love life so they can gossip about it with other people. I'm talking about the neighbor who always asks you to do last-minute favors for them with no regard to whether or not you actually have the time.

Then of course there are the neighbors who play their music as loud as they want at night and allow their dogs to bark for hours on end during the day with no regard to the disruption it has on your life.

How about siblings? Do you have a brother or sister who lives their life exactly as they choose, while continually making judgmental remarks about how you choose to live YOUR life?

I could go on, but I'm sure in a matter of seconds you can reflect on your life and mentally expand on my list. Again, boundary violations in your personal life may not seem too dramatic on the surface. But over time they can eat away at you, drain your energy, and waste a ton of time.

Are you currently putting up with violations of your personal boundaries? If so, why? Are you afraid to rock the boat? Are you someone who'll do almost anything to avoid confrontation?

Think for a moment about people who are violating your personal boundaries, and ask yourself why you're putting up with it. You don't have to write anything yet, but feel free to take a glance over at your pen and journal ... because you're going to need it soon.

Relationship Boundaries

This is the big one. Establishing boundaries with your spouse or partner has been the subject of countless books, movies, blogs, videos, webinars, seminars, and multi-module online programs. This topic is a multi-million dollar cottage industry in itself. But I'm only going to give it a few paragraphs, because I know that as you read this your mind is already writing pages on the topic.

For starters, are you being given the time and space you need in your relationship to be YOU? Or, has this boundary been violated to the point where your partner expects his or her needs to be your first priority?

If you're a woman of a certain age, you're aware that women were taught to accept "the fact" that their needs and desires were secondary to the needs of their husband. And when I say second, I mean a distant second! Conversely, many men have been conditioned by society to believe that the financial cost of dates, dinners, monthly bills, and weekend getaways is their responsibility.

Fortunately, today we live in a culture that stresses greater equality between men and women. This is a positive trend that remains a continual work in progress. The result of greater equality between partners means that outdated traditional roles within a relationship are gradually falling to the wayside. Hooray for this!

However, this also means that roles within a relationship must be discussed between couples and this requires open and honest conversations about personal boundaries that pertain to careers, hobbies, friendships, health and wellness, and the space you need just to be YOU as an individual.

Remember, equality means EQUAL, which means your personal boundaries are as important as your partner's. So use this moment as you read to be aware of boundaries in your relationship that you may be allowing your partner to trample on. And, ask yourself if there are areas where you're not being completely respectful of your partner's boundaries.

Health Boundaries

Nothing is more important than your health! In fact, as I write this it is February of 2021 and the U.S. and countries around the world are in the midst of the COVID-19 virus pandemic. Other than essential workers, many people in the United States are being asked to stay at home to avoid contracting and spreading the virus. Scary stuff, and the ultimate example of why nothing is more important than your health.

As part of dealing with the COVID-19 pandemic, every American is being asked to practice *social distancing*, which requires you to stay at least six feet away from other individuals. This requires you to set a literal health boundary that you must strictly enforce to avoid contracting a disease that can make you very sick and even kill you.

Since COVID-19 is a worldwide pandemic, I'm going to assume you have firsthand experience with the extreme measures that I've just described. I'm also going to assume that you learned several valuable lessons during the pandemic.

One of which is the importance of setting health boundaries. If you took social distancing measures during the pandemic and washed your hands 15 times a day, you did it because you loved yourself enough to take the necessary measures to minimize the chance of becoming ill.

Even though you may no longer be dealing with a pandemic, it's still vital to establish health-related boundaries in your day-to-day life. They may not need to be as extreme as those you established during the COVID-19 crisis, but they are equally as important and the foundation for these boundaries should be rooted in unconditional self-love.

Health boundaries may not be something you think about in everyday life, but establishing them is essential. Here's why:

Remember, people will often try to project their health habits onto you. If you eat a healthy whole foods diet to maintain a lean body, you may have to deal with people who refer to you as being "too skinny." When this happens, take a good look at the person making this comment. Chances are, they may be carrying too much weight as a result of having some unresolved issues with their own eating habits.

I have friends who avoid eating sugar, which means they never eat cake or cookies or ice cream. As a result, these friends tell me that they have to deal with other people making judgmental remarks to them along the lines of, "You shouldn't be so strict about what you eat because you're depriving yourself."

Well, *deprivation* is a relative term. While some people may feel they are depriving themselves by not eating sweet, tasty cake or cookies, other people may feel the only things they're depriving themselves of are love handles and heart disease.

Here is another example. If you don't drink, who is most likely to give you flak about it when you're at a party or social gathering? Probably someone who could stand to drink a little less.

Who is most likely to give you some ribbing about your frequent trips to the gym and your desire to keep your body fit and attractive? Probably someone who wishes they were in better shape.

It's an odd phenomenon, but for some reason many people choose to project their health issues onto others. Your response to this should be to set firm health boundaries, and love and respect yourself enough to enforce them. Why? Because without your health, you ain't got a damn thing!

Setting Boundaries Trains People

When you are firm about setting boundaries, a magical thing happens: people become conditioned and trained to respect them. Here is a simple example:

I used to work with a website developer who did great work in a timely manner. She had a boundary in her business in which she was very clear that she'd respond to my emails within 24 "business" hours. This meant that if I emailed her on Tuesday at 2 p.m. I would expect to receive a response from her by Wednesday at 2 p.m.

However, if I emailed her on Friday at 2 p.m., I might not hear from her until Monday at 2 p.m. She was very clear that she didn't email or conduct meetings at night or on weekends. She never made an exception to these boundaries and I respected that because she always did great work.

So, if I emailed her Wednesday at 2 p.m., I didn't expect to hear from her until the next day. If I emailed her on Friday, I just assumed I wouldn't receive a response until Monday. She loved and respected herself enough to establish and enforce these boundaries. By doing so, she trained and conditioned me to respect her boundaries.

Now, if I emailed her at 4 p.m. on a Tuesday and she established a pattern by which she responded back to me by 7 p.m. that night, I probably would have expected her to always respond to my emails within a few hours, regardless of when I sent them.

Instead, she established a firm boundary of responding to emails within 24 business hours. By loving and respecting herself to never waiver on this boundary, she trained and conditioned me to respect it.

Think about your life. Are there areas where people have conditioned you to accept and respect their boundaries? I imagine there are.

Now ask yourself if there are areas in your life where you need to establish strong, unwavering boundaries that people need to be trained and conditioned to respect. If you're like me, this is an aspect of your life that probably needs some work.

So grab your pen and pad, and let's get to it!

Your Journaling Power Prompt

Pick at least three areas of your life where you need to establish stronger boundaries. You can choose more, but I want you to pick at least three. Remember, no one is going to read your journal except you. So don't hold back.

Give this some thought and then let loose. As you write your list, be as sharp and as specific as you can. For example, don't just write "I need to set strong boundaries with some people at work." Instead, write your entry with more depth and substance, as in this example:

> *"I need to set a boundary with Greg at work, because he comes into my office several times a week to stir up drama and talk about office politics. His negative attitude drains my energy and his interruptions waste my time and kill the positive momentum I have going with my projects."*

Whether you're listing boundary issues that relate to work, your health, your wealth, or your personal relationships, be detailed and specific with your writing.

After you've written about at least three areas of your life where you need to establish strong boundaries, here's what I want you to do next.

For each of these three areas, write down how committed you are to enforcing these boundaries no matter what, so others will become trained and conditioned to respect them. Be firm and certain as you write. In addition, paint a picture with your words that describes in vivid detail how different your life will look and feel with these boundaries firmly in place.

Remember, the foundation of each of these new boundaries is the unconditional love and respect you feel for yourself. So if you want to take this journaling prompt a step further, detail how the unconditional love you feel for yourself will make it easier for you to enforce these boundaries when they are challenged. Because they will be challenged. When this happens, stand strong and love yourself!

Chapter 7

Focus on Joy and Laughter

After reading the first six chapters of *Mindset Medicine* you should feel the momentum building in your soul. I'm going to trust at this point that you've followed through on all of our journaling prompts. If you haven't, please go back and complete them, because doing so will make you feel fantastic!

If you've completed them, I have a big gift for you in this chapter. The gift of laughter!

As you've probably heard, laughter is the best medicine. What you may not have heard is that it's so much easier to tap into this never-ending FREE supply of medicine when you love and respect yourself without conditions and when you have established firm boundaries in your life that you defend with confidence and certainty.

Think about it. When you love and respect yourself, you walk with a bounce in your step. When you walk with a bounce in your step, you tend to be more happy. When you're more happy, you tend to gravitate toward joy and laughter.

Unfortunately, our society, coupled with how our bodies are hardwired, often make it difficult to seek out joy and laughter because ...

... Serious and Scared Is Our Default Setting

This is a topic I touched on earlier, but it's worth revisiting because it has such a powerful influence in your life.

For better and for worse, humans are hard-wired to be serious and fearful. This is because a long time ago we lived in caves, and we had to leave those caves each day to gather food. Sounds like a leisurely life compared to now. The problem was that there were animals outside those caves who wanted to make us *their* next meal.

Because of this, people needed to be focused, leery, and on edge in order to sense when danger was around the corner. Being scared and a little paranoid had its benefits. Being scared meant being alert, and being alert meant you at least had a fighting chance when the lions and bears snuck up behind you.

Now, were there happy-go-lucky people back then? Were there people who focused on joy and laughter? Probably. But they probably met their demise outside of the cave quicker than those who were more serious, fearful, and focused on what could go wrong. In other words, the serious and scared people probably avoided death by animal better than the happy-go-lucky crowd.

As a result of this "survival of the fittest" pattern, being serious and scared became hardwired into our DNA. Bottom line, being serious and fearful is how we protect ourselves. This is why most people tend to fear the unseen and the unknown when they could instead appreciate the seen and known that's right in front of them.

While being scared and serious keeps you safe, this underlying thread running through your DNA can work against you. This is unfortunate, because in today's society you are safer than you've ever been, so being scared and fearful isn't as necessary as it once was.

Then why do we spend so much time still being frightened by what life has in store for us? Maybe it's because ...

... Modern Society Has New Ways of Scaring the Hell Out of Us!

Today, instead of starting their day by leaving their cave to collect food, millions of people turn on their TV and check their email moments after they awake. If you're among the growing legions of people who are choosing instead to meditate and/or journal first thing in the morning, good for you!

However, even if we choose to ease our way into it, at some point each day the avalanche of e-sludge begins to beat down on us. Sadly, in today's society, 24-hour news, social media, and our email inboxes have replaced lions and tigers and bears, oh my! Making matters worse is that the bulk of the messages we receive through the media are negative to the point of scaring the hell out of us each and every day.

Today, tuning into the world through 24-hour news means being exposed to endless argumentative messages about politics, cyber attacks, identity theft, China, Russia, sex scandals, bigotry, racism, sexism, and the fact that you may not be saving enough for retirement, which means you may outlive your money and find yourself homeless when you're 92 years old!

It seems that everything you hear these days is designed to activate the fear "mechanism" within you that was originally intended to protect you from being eaten by wild animals.

Are there people who are immune to such negative distractions in their lives? Of course there are. In fact, many of the happiest people I know are those who don't have any idea what's going on in the world! I'm sure you know people like this too. But what do we typically say about these people? Well, we often criticize them for having "their heads buried in the sand." Maybe we should instead model their behavior, because maybe they know something we don't!

Now, I'm not suggesting you ignore what's going on in the world completely. But I do suggest that you take notice of the fact that at least 95% of what you hear on TV each day, especially cable news, isn't actually going on in your immediate surrounding area or affecting your daily routine all that much.

Most of the bad things we hear about each day through the media are occurring somewhere far away or are "potentially" going to happen to us many years down the road. Yet, we still allow them to drain our energy and alter our mood in a negative way. This is because most of what you hear on TV and other media outlets revolves around drama and conflict. Why? Because drama and conflict sell!

This is evident by the fact that every news broadcast almost always features bad news and all of the drama, arguing, and conflict that goes with it. Very rarely does the news media feature good news and the happiness that goes with it. And when it does, it's presented to you during the last two minutes of a news broadcast before they invite you to tune in again tomorrow so they can fill your mind with more bad news, conflict, and drama. It's an endless cycle, and if you pay too much attention to it you're going to find it very difficult, if not impossible, to focus on joy and laughter.

Here's how I see it. When you're on your deathbed, you may look back on your life and feel regret for not having spent enough time laughing and feeling joyful. However, I think I can say with certainty that you're not going to feel regret for not having watched enough 24-hour news and all of the stress, tension, and arguing that goes with it.

As if the never-ending 24-hour scary news cycle isn't enough, modern technology has now made it extremely cheap and easy for you to own a handheld "clutter-your-brain-with-endless distractions" device, which we innocently call our *cell phone.*

Between the emails, texts, and social media posts pulsating through your cell phone, it's easy to feel as if you're in a constant state of agitation and distraction. And even though you're being continually bombarded with messages through your phone, it's equally as easy to feel as though you're missing out on something.

The end result of all this is that, for many people, only miniscule amounts of time are spent focused on joy and laughter. Can you relate to this feeling? If you can, keep reading! Because the simple solution to this problem is to make joy and laughter a big priority in your life. Here's how you do it.

Ask Yourself Two Life-Transforming Questions

Before I share two simple questions that will change your life, I want you to consider the fact that all you really have is the moment you're living in right NOW. You can't relive your past. You can learn plenty of lessons from it for sure, but you can't relive it.

You can think about the future and prepare for it, but you can't live in the future. And the truth is, at best you can only have a vague idea about what's really going to happen in the future. So don't worry about how things are going to be too far down the road because the future is too hard to predict. The way we were all blindsided by the COVID-19 pandemic and all of the abrupt changes it caused in our lives is a perfect example.

Given that the future is so hard to predict accurately, focus most of your thoughts on NOW because NOW is all you really have. After you get yourself focused on what you are doing now, ask yourself these two simple but life-transforming questions:

1. What's funny about the situation I'm in right now?
2. How can I make the situation I'm in right now a 10?

That's it. All you have to do is ask yourself what's funny about any given situation, and all you have to do is ask yourself how you can make the situation you're in right now a #10 experience on a scale of one to 10. If you can train yourself to do this and make this mindset your new default setting, it will completely transform your life.

Can you transition to this mindset overnight? Probably not. But you can certainly do it over time.

Do you think this is unrealistic? Maybe you do, maybe you don't. But here's how you can begin this transformation.

Take a moment and consider how good you really have it. Remember, unlike your long-lost and forgotten relatives, you don't have to worry about lions and tigers and bears as you venture out to gather food each day.

Instead, you merely have to crawl out of your comfortable bed in your climate-controlled home and open your refrigerator to get food. If you don't immediately turn on the TV and/or check your email, you should be able to find a little fun and humor in this routine.

Here's another perspective to consider.

Think about your favorite comedians for a moment, anyone from Jerry Seinfeld to Chris Rock and everyone in between. Now consider the foundation for all of their stand-up comedy routines. More often than not, it's observational humor. Great comedians continually look for the "what's-funny-about-this?" factor in every moment they observe. They then focus on how they can take their observations and turn them into comedy bits that allow them to give their audience a #10 entertainment experience.

Comedians live in this mindset. They've trained themselves to look at the world through this prism. Sure, Jerry Seinfeld and Chris Rock are quite wealthy and can afford to look at the world from this humorous point of view. But the fact is, they perfected this mindset when they were dead broke, and that's what made them wealthy. Proof that focusing on joy and laughter can really pay off!

Another example comes from *Create Write Now* tribe member Casey Demchak who took acting classes when he attended Loyola Marymount University in Los Angeles,

California. In one of his classes, Casey and a few of his classmates were required to perform a dramatic scene from the classic play, *Death of a Salesman*, written by Arthur Miller.

Casey and his fellow actors rehearsed the scene numerous times and then performed it in front of the class. The instructor asked them to perform the dramatic scene six different times until they got it just right. Then he looked at Casey and his fellow actors and said, "That was great. Now do the same scene as a comedy without changing any of the dialogue."

Casey tells me that, at first, he and the other actors were completely caught off guard. They didn't know what to do. But then they glanced between each other, put smiles on their faces, adjusted their body language and the timing and delivery of their lines … and they did the scene as a comedy. And it worked!

They had fun and got a few laughs, but what Casey said he learned was that when you put your mind to it you really can make almost any "dramatic" situation light and fun in the spur of a moment. All it takes is a sudden shift in your focus, posture, and mindset.

Now, it may be hard to laugh when a loved one is dying or a tornado is bearing down on your house. But overall in the course of your daily life, you certainly have the power to change your attitude rather quickly and make joy and laughter your default mentality, instead of living in a state of stress, drama, and tension.

Journaling is a great way to make this transition in your life!

Your Journaling Power Prompt

Grab your journal and pen, and write down at least three recurring patterns or routines in your daily life that typically make you feel stressed or distracted. Given all of the noise we have in our day-to-day lives, this should be pretty easy to do.

However, give this some thought and pick at least three patterns or routines that seem to impact your life the most. Perhaps it's the stress you feel each morning when you try to get your sleepy kids out of bed so they can get ready for school. Maybe it's the mind-numbing grind of your daily drive to work. Or maybe it's the stress you feel when you return from work to a chaotic household or a lonely apartment.

We all have mental patterns in our lives. We all have recurring thoughts we typically connect to patterns of activity we repeat throughout the week. You may not be able abruptly to change your daily or weekly routines, but you can certainly interrupt and change the thought patterns you reflexively associate with these recurring activities.

After giving it some thought, write down three recurring patterns or routines in your life that tend to stress you out, make you unhappy, or just fill your mind with negative energy-draining thoughts.

For each of these three patterns or routines, ask yourself these two questions: 1) What can I do to make this situation humorous? And 2) What can I do to make this situation a 10?

Now, write down exactly how you intend to bring some levity to these three patterns, and craft some ideas about how you can make each of these recurring routines or patterns a 10 … or as close to a 10 as you can.

For example, maybe your slow bumper-to-bumper commute each day is a great chance to "people watch" other drivers stuck in traffic as you listen to stand-up comedy audio. Maybe the chaos of coming home to your kids is a chance to repeat some of the jokes you heard during your commute, so you can replace their complaining with laughter. Perhaps coming home to an empty apartment is the ideal time to start a daily meditation routine.

Remember, all you have is NOW. If you have pretty good health and you're not being chased by a wild animal, your life isn't all that bad. This means that most every situation can be turned into a positive moment that is upbeat and at least a little humorous.

However, this can only happen if you shift your focus and ask how you can make a given situation FUN. So, identify three recurring patterns in your life and write down exactly how you intend to make them more lighthearted and enjoyable.

Doing this may seem like a challenge at first given how programmed we are by society to be so damn serious all the time. However, if you do the necessary work to make this shift in your mindset, the positivity it will bring to your soul will be life-changing.

I understand it may take time to master this new mindset, so it might be wise to do (or to review and revise) this journaling exercise each day until you begin to feel a daily dose of levity flow through your veins.

When you get in a jam, you may want to remember the example I gave you of when fellow journaling revolutionary Casey Demchak and his acting classmates were told to turn the dramatic scene they performed into a comedy.

You can do the same in real life too. When you do, it will make it so much easier for you to stay in the moment and focus on joy and laughter!

Chapter 8

Gratitude and Pivoting to Better-Feeling Thoughts

The easiest way to live a life in which you focus on joy and laughter is to embrace an attitude of gratitude and appreciation. And of course, the most important thing in the world on which to focus your appreciation is YOU!

In terms of the vibe you put out to the Universe, gratitude and love are said to be identical. This makes sense, because when you love someone you appreciate them. When you love something, you appreciate it.

Most important, when you feel love and appreciation for anybody, anything, or any moment … you feel good. And when you feel good it is so much easier to focus on joy and laughter. Plus, I am certain you and I were put on this planet to spend as much time as possible feeling good. Talk about mindset medicine!

No one has ever laid on their deathbed regretting the time in life they spent feeling good. It is your birthright to feel good. What's truly amazing is that you have within you the power to choose better-feeling thoughts at any given moment.

The most basic thought you can choose anytime day or night is how much you love yourself. I say slather it on as thick as you can!

In the last chapter, I talked about how all you really have is right NOW. Well, right now you have the power to choose a better-feeling thought by simply thinking about something you appreciate. The more time you spend appreciating yourself, other people, and beautiful things, the more time you'll spend feeling happy.

It really isn't any more complicated than this. This should be all the reason you need to look for things throughout the day to love and to appreciate. It's also a fantastic reason to journal every day about things you appreciate.

When you fill your being with a sense of appreciation and love, which you can always do, you will feel happy. So do it. Remember, the best things in life are free, which means your ability to feel happy and joyful at all times is an incredible bargain.

No doubt you've heard this before, but it really is good for your overall health and happiness to live with an attitude of gratitude. When you feel gratitude, love, and appreciation for things, it's much easier to allow joy and laughter to flow with reckless abandon through your soul.

Now, I know you may be thinking, "Ok, Mari. I know it's good to live with an attitude of gratitude. I've heard this before. But it's not always easy to spend my day looking for little things to appreciate it."

If you ever feel this way, I can relate. Remember, I have Multiple Sclerosis! So I know it can be a struggle to ALWAYS find things to appreciate about it. I get it. I know from my own life experience that sometimes it can feel like living with an attitude of gratitude is something you almost have to force yourself to do. I know it can be a challenge to keep an attitude-of-gratitude hour after hour or week after week.

However, I do have a handy tool that makes it much easier for you to sustain your appreciation groove. This is another life tool that is free of charge and at your disposal anytime day or night. It's a lot of fun to play with, and it makes it significantly easier for you to remain in an ongoing state of joy and appreciation.

To use this tool all you have to do is ...

... Focus Your Thoughts on What Makes You Feel Good!

I love this topic, because it is so near and dear to my soul. I can summarize it in just a few words: It's okay to feel good all the time! In fact, you are on this Earth to feel good all the time.

If you struggle with this concept even just a little, I suggest you make this phrase the first thing you write in your journal each day. I'll say it again - It's okay to feel good all the time!

This is such a simple and powerful lesson to learn, because you may have been raised to believe that good things only come to you through toil, struggle, and hard work. Think back to how you felt as a child as your mom or dad walked with you through the toy section of the department store.

How did that make you feel? I'm going to go out on a limb and say it made you feel incredible. Remember how you felt like you were walking on air? Remember the smile on your face? Remember how energized you felt? All because you were literally bathing in a sea of guilt-free-unapologetically-easy-breezy thoughts.

Give yourself permission to go back to this feeling every day of your life!

Tell yourself your natural state is one in which you feel great. Go ahead and put a big grin on your face and think of something that makes you feel good. Being in a joyous state of embracing good thoughts releases all resistance and makes it so much easier for joy, laughter, and fun to flow through your life.

This is how you are meant to live!

As a child, thinking about things that were fun and exciting came so natural to you, and it made you feel amazing. Thinking fun thoughts and feeling good inside is the clearest indicator that you are in alignment with who you really are.

When you want things you feel good. When you appreciate things and people you feel good. Feeling good is how you were meant to feel. As a small child you knew this intuitively, and that is why you endlessly looked for and invented ways to create joy and laughter in your life.

It wasn't until you became a young adult that you began to struggle with thoughts about whether you were *worthy* or *deserving* of something. It wasn't until older adults taught you that life was about toil and pain that you began to brood and think negative thoughts that took you out of alignment with who you really are.

Well, I'm here to tell you: now that you're a bigger kid, it's still okay to want things and think about things that make you feel great. Who cares whether you are worthy or deserving of more money, or a better job, or your ideal lover? Whenever you question whether you're worthy or deserving of something, it makes you feel lousy, which creates vibrational resistance in your life.

As we learned in chapter four, the way to override this state is through the sheer vibrational power of wanting! The delightful state of joyous wanting easily tramples over the weakened vibrational state you sink into when you have an inner debate about whether you're worthy, good enough, or deserving of something.

And, the best thing about wanting is that wanting makes you feel great. When you feel negative thoughts that make you feel crappy or angry inside, the quickest way to pivot to feeling better is to take a deep breath and daydream about things you want. Do this, and it will make you feel fantastic. And when you feel fantastic, that which you desire comes to you with much greater ease.

I am certain there is no greater skill than the ability continuously to focus your thoughts on what you want. I encourage you to be incredibly childlike with this skill. Let it rip. When you put yourself in a joyous state of wanting you put out an unstoppable vibration that makes it so much easier to smother your soul with unconditional self-love.

Again, I want you to be super childlike with this skill. Feel the continuous happiness that comes with wanting things or thinking back in your life about fun things you've done. Nobody even has to know you're doing this all day long. It can be your secret. You can just walk around with a big silly grin on your face as you want your way through each and every day. People will feel the positive vibes emanating from your heart and they'll be dying to know how you do it.

Reconnect with the power of wanting, daydreaming, and imagining that you wielded like a mighty sword when you were a child. Doing this doesn't make you selfish. Rather, it makes you feel incredible and it frees you to send out a powerful vibration the Universe is dying to respond to.

So go for it! WANT things, appreciate things, imagine a wonderful life story for yourself. Learn to pivot to better-feeling thoughts at any given moment throughout your day!

Focus on Telling Better-Feeling Self-Stories

Giving yourself permission to focus your thoughts on telling a new life story is a powerful way to keep yourself in an energizing frame of mind that attracts great things into your life like a magnet. A wonderful way to further fuel this energy is to tell your story as if it's already happened.

For example, don't tell a story about the new dream job you'd like to attract into your life. Instead, tell the story of how it feels to <u>already have</u> this dream job. Go into detail about the higher salary you're making. Talk about the new friends you've made through your new position. Go into vivid detail about how happy it makes you feel to have a career in which you are able fully to utilize your talents and gifts.

Be affirmative with your storytelling. Act and feel as if the story you'd like to see come true for yourself has already happened.

Do this, and it will make you feel fantastic. When you feel fantastic, the self-love flows and all that you desire comes to you with much less resistance!

With a little practice you can get really good at this. Paint a beautiful proactive picture in your mind of how your life looks and feels now that you've welcomed what you desire into your life.

Your journal is a wonderful place to record your affirmative self-stories. Nobody else has to know the pleasurable state you're putting yourself in by telling such affirmative stories about your life. And don't hold anything back. Be big and bold with your reasons for wanting what you want. Make no apologies. Just go for it!

Do you want to improve your health and get in better physical shape? Write a fanciful story about how good it feels now that you can buy clothes to show off your body instead of cover it up.

Do you want to grow your business and generate greater revenues? Tell yourself a fun-filled story about a relaxing weekend you just spent in a mountain cabin that sits on the edge of beautiful hot springs. All paid for by the additional money you're now making.

Do you want to meet your soulmate and new best friend? Tell yourself the story of the great time you had with them when they joined you on your trip to the mountain cabin by the hot springs.

Worthy and deserving of what you desire? Who cares, just WANT it, and tell yourself a proactive story of how good it feels to have it already.

Give yourself permission to want with all your heart and feel certain that what you want has already come into your life. Act and feel as if what you desire most is at your fingertips right NOW.

Enjoy this feeling and nourish it. This will put you in an incredible state of receiving that empowers you to love yourself and turn everyday moments into wondrous events.

Again, putting yourself in this frame of mind came natural to you as a child. Rediscover this gift and put it back to work for you NOW. When you do, laughter and joy will fill your life and unconditional self-love will fill your heart.

You can do this! Grab your pen and journal, and let's make it happen!

Your Journaling Power Prompt

This journaling prompt is going to be fun. What I want you to do is put a big grin across your face, put yourself in a childlike state, and don't hold back anything. Let it go and have fun with this!

Grab your journal and make a list of at least five things you really WANT. It could be anything. More money, a better job, a great relationship, better health, a new car, a better wardrobe. Don't limit yourself and don't be "realistic."

Dream and think big like you did when you were a kid!

Next, write down how good it feels to already have each of these five things. Don't worry about sounding self-centered or all about you. In fact, go ahead and be all about YOU! Just let loose and write from your heart. Have fun with this. The more honest, open, and enthusiastic you are with this prompt, the better you are going to feel.

And, don't forget to keep a great big grin on your face as you're writing! Just let loose and write about each of your five things as if you already have them. Tell the story of how nice it feels to possess each of these five things. Think, feel, and act as if they are already yours!

This is called affirmative journaling. When you write, feel, and act as if you already have that which you desire, you put a magnetic vibration out to the Universe and that's when magic happens in your life.

Again, have fun with this journaling prompt. Go back to being a kid; put a great big smile on your face ... and go for it!

Chapter 9

Celebrate Being a Hero for Others

Over the last several chapters, you and I have focused on developing the inner YOU. We've delved deeply into the importance of demanding respect from others, setting boundaries, and establishing a positive mindset that allows joy and laughter to come into your life with much more ease.

In this chapter, I'm going to give you a chance to turn outward and do an exercise that will continue to make you feel great about yourself. This exercise, and the lesson you'll gain from it, may be something you've never done before to the extent that you're going to in this chapter.

What I'll ask you to do over the next few pages is to breathe deeply, relax, and examine all the nice things you've done for others. I have no doubt you've done BIG things for people during the course of your life and you should celebrate them.

However, in this chapter I'm going to have you look at the little and often unnoticed things you do on a daily basis that you may give little or no thought to. The gift of doing this exercise is that by the end of this chapter you'll feel more empowered and have even more reasons than you already do to love yourself unconditionally.

You Are a Hero!

Make no doubt about it. You are a hero to others in more ways than you can imagine, and you should love yourself for this.

For example, a simple trip to the grocery store where you spend money on a regular basis helps keep the people who work there employed.

The smile you give to the cashier and the small talk you make with the person bagging your groceries make their day more pleasant and enjoyable. When you come home from the store and park in front of your home, there may be an elderly person walking past that you know in your neighborhood. The friendly hello and the casual comment you make to them about the weather may be the only conversation that person has with someone all day. The next time they walk past your home, they may be hoping to see you outside again.

When you pay your bills each month, as painful as this can be, you are contributing to the wellbeing of your community by circulating money so others can maintain their dreams of living a fulfilling life. A friendly hello, the routine act of buying food, paying your bills, or making sure your pet has a bowl of fresh water are simple acts that make you a hero and a key contributor to the wellness of others.

You should love yourself for these small things and little moments and never take them for granted. To help you do this I've outlined six areas of your life in which you are probably more heroic on a daily basis than you realize.

You're a Hero for Your Partner and Children

The greatest thing you're doing right now to be a hero for your partner is learning to love yourself more. Even if you were madly in love with yourself before, the fact that you're smack dab in the middle of this book means you're committed to loving yourself even more.

You're a hero because you're invested in loving yourself. When you're invested in loving yourself, it is infinitely easier for others to love you, and it is infinitely easier to give love to others in a way that is heartfelt and genuine.

Before every commercial airline flight, the flight attendant tells you that in the event of a loss of cabin pressure, those yellow masks will pop out. You're then told to secure YOUR mask first before you try to help others secure theirs. The point being that you won't be of much use to anyone else if you can't breathe. By securing your own mask first, you make it possible to help others who are struggling.

The same can be said about self-love and your relationship with your partner and your children. By taking the time to put YOU first, you are creating a core foundation within your soul that empowers you to be a rock-solid hero for your partner and children.

The simple fact that you care enough to do this means you can be a hero to them in every aspect of their lives. In our culture, we're often taught to be selfless and think of our partner and our children first. But ignoring your own needs makes you weak and less stable, and it's hard to be a rock for others if inside you're on the brink of crumbling.

However, when you put yourself first and shore up your physical and emotional foundation, you're in a much stronger position to be there for your partner and children when they need you. And they always need you. If you have the courage to realize this and put loving yourself ahead of all else, you're more heroic than you can imagine.

Now, if you're single you may not feel as though you are a hero for a partner or children you may not have, but you certainly are a hero for others in your life.

You're a Hero for Your Friends

When was the last time you were called by a friend who wanted to share a success story with you or discuss a challenge they were facing. It's easy to take it for granted that you have friends, but each time one of them calls YOU to discuss issues in their tissues they do so for a simple reason. You mean something to them. They see you as someone who cares about them. They see you as someone they can count on.

When you listen to your friends and give of yourself during times of need and times of celebration, you're being a hero for them. When you laugh with them, listen to their concerns, or lend them a hand when they need to fix, repair, or move something in their home, you're being a hero.

Although it's easy to think of your friends as people who are always "there," never underestimate the important role you play in their lives and how much you mean to them.

You're a Superhero in Your Pet's Eyes

Pets bring you unconditional love 24 hours a day, seven days a week. Cuddling with your cat or petting and hugging your dog can immediately soothe your nerves and bring you a sense of calm. You gain so much from your pets, and there isn't anything you wouldn't do to care for them, to protect them, and to give them a comfortable and happy life.

How often do you stop to consider what a superhero you are to your pets? How often do you stop and think about the wonderful things you do for them that would be so much more challenging for them to do for themselves?

For example, if you've rescued a dog from a shelter, removed him from a cage and a life of fear, and given him a stable home, you've done something gracious and heroic in his eyes. And your ability to flip lids and operate faucets that keep your dog supplied with food and water all day is an incredible talent for which he'll always be grateful.

Add in that skill you possess to fine-tune the air conditioner when it's 90 degrees in the summer, and you'll understand why in your pet's eyes you are a true superstar.

You're a Hero in Your Community

The simple act of going on a walk in your neighborhood, whether you're alone or with your partner or pet, can make you a hero in your community. Think of the people you pass by as you walk. Some you just may wave to; others may be people you stop and chat with for a bit as they sit on their front porch. These may be people you don't go out and socialize with, but your steady presence in the neighborhood brings a sense of calm and normalcy to their lives.

The elderly couple that sits together on their porch in the early evening may look forward to seeing you pass by because the brief conversation you have with them brightens your day. If you walk your dog in the early evening, you no doubt encounter other dog walkers who, along with their dogs, are familiar faces. Their short chat with you each night might be what takes the edge off of a busy, hectic day.

The paved roads and street signs that you take for granted during your walk? All paid for by the taxes you pay when you buy goods and services in your community. Do you donate blood, volunteer for an animal shelter, or do some work for your homeowner's association?

All of these little actions that bring a sense of comfort and fulfillment to your life also brings peace and stability to many others. Your daily routines within your community make you an everyday hero to others in ways you probably rarely think about. But you should, and you should love yourself for it.

You're a Hero at Work

For some it's drudgery and for others it's a joy. But work is part of nearly all of our lives. If you're reading this book, I feel confident in assuming you either view your work as joyful creation or you are in the process of manifesting a lifestyle that empowers you to make the most of the gifts you have to share with the world.

As you share these gifts, it's important to consider the positive ripple effect your words and actions have on the lives of others. It's hard to give examples because there are millions of different types of vocations in the world. However, what most of them have in common is that they exist to help others in some way.

All too often, we only think of our work as something we do to earn money so we can pay our bills and make a living.

But I'd like you to reflect on your work and think about the positive impact it is making right now in the lives of others.

Really think this one through. Consider the simple actions you take each day through your work and visualize how they travel on down the line, touching the lives of others while providing them with something they need right now or something that adds long-term value to their lives.

Every job has a positive ripple effect in the world. Take a few moments to follow the ripple you create with yours. Then take a minute to love and appreciate yourself, because the ripple you generate each and every day makes you a hero to everyone who is touched by it.

You're a Wealth-Building Hero

It's easy to become stressed on those days when you have to hop in your car and run a series of errands that require you to spend money at the market, the dry cleaner, or the clothing store. However, instead of focusing on how much traffic there is or the time crunch you're under, you may choose to think about how you're circulating money so others can make a living so that they, too, can spend money that helps others make a living.

It's easy to think of "the economy" as a distant, convoluted set of numbers that are tied to Wall Street, the stock market, and other "leading economic indicators" that are difficult to understand. But the fact is, "the economy" is YOU running your errands and circulating money so that others in your community can keep a roof over their heads and food in their refrigerators.

Believe it or not, you are a living, breathing economic engine for others. You should recognize this and be proud of it. Paying your bills, buying your groceries, treating yourself to a meal at a restaurant, or hanging out in your local coffee shop empowers others to make a living so that they can pursue their hopes and dreams.

In your own simple day-to-day way, YOU are a wealth-building hero for yourself and others, and this is yet another aspect of yourself you should admire and celebrate.

Your Journaling Power Prompt

Look at the six areas of your life I outlined above. You can also consider other areas unique to your life that I didn't mention. Pick at least three of these areas, and write a page that describes in detail how you have been a hero for others.

Don't be too modest and rush through this. You are more of a hero to others than you'll ever know. You contribute in positive, uplifting ways to the lives of more people than you realize. Now is the time to recognize this heroism and honor yourself.

Do you feel a little silly doing this exercise? Well, you shouldn't. Just think of all the time you've spent in front of a mirror during your life beating up on yourself for what you perceive as your imperfections. If you've taken the time to do this (*and we all have*) then you can certainly take some time to honor and recognize the multifaceted hero that is YOU!

Again, pick three or more areas of your life and write at least a page on each. Detail the big things and little things you do each day that, even in some small measure, contribute to the greater good of someone else's life.

Breathe and enjoy this exercise as you move through it. Smile and dig deep as you realize the glorious things you do in so many areas of your life that have an important ripple effect throughout your home, your community, and the planet.

Now comes the wonderful part. And promise me you'll do this! After you've written your pages, stand in front of a mirror and read them aloud as you look at yourself and love yourself for the amazing things, big and small, you do for the world around you.

You truly are a hero in so many ways and today is the day to honor this fact and bask in its glory!

Chapter 10

What Do You Promise to Do
to Be YOUR Hero?

Now that you've become crystal clear about the fact that you are a hero to others, you and I are going to turn the attention back to YOU in this chapter. This is going to be fun, because I'm going to inspire you to pamper yourself.

I'd say that you deserve and are worthy of being pampered, but you know how I feel about being deserving or worthy of things. It isn't necessary. All you have to do ... and say it loud and proud with me ... is to WANT to pamper yourself.

The main point here is: when you take the time to realize what a hero you are to others, it's perfectly fine to commit to being an even greater hero to yourself. Besides, the bigger and better you are as a hero for YOU, the better you can be as a hero for others.

In this chapter, I want you to pamper yourself by making a list of things you promise to do to be YOUR greatest hero. And remember, heroes think BIG. So I want you to really go for it and have fun with this. Together, you and I are going to look at essential areas of your life, and I'm going to ask you to make promises to yourself about the wonderful things you are committed to doing to be your own hero!

This of course is going to lead to a really fun journaling prompt. But first, let's set the stage by taking a close look at key areas of your life and addressing some potential issues in your tissues.

Flow Downstream Instead of Upstream

Before you determine how you can be more of a hero to YOU, I want to create a positive vibration for yourself. All too often when we examine different areas of our life, we're asked by "the experts" to look at what's "wrong" with our lives and decide what we're willing to do to "fix" it.

The problem with this approach is that it never feels good inside. In fact, right out of the gate it makes you feel crappy because it's implied that parts of you are broken. You may have issues in your tissues as we all do, but I can assure you that you're certainly not broken.

What's fundamentally wrong with the "fix it" approach is that it creates an uncomfortable angst within you, which promotes a mental struggle that makes you feel as if you're swimming upstream against the current. Feeling this way is the surest indicator that it's time to change your mindset because you are meant to feel GOOD. When you feel good, you have an inner sense that you are in a positive vibrational flow that feels as if you're swimming downstream with the current—not against it.

Perhaps this is the first promise you can make to yourself about what you're willing to do to be YOUR own hero. Promise to recognize that you should always mentally feel as though you are swimming downstream with the current, which is always a more pleasant state of mind in which to be.

So go ahead, make this promise to YOU right now as you joyously look at the following key areas of your life. Also, promise yourself right now that you'll never think of yourself as being broken and in need of repair. Instead, make a pledge that you'll always look at yourself as being a blessed and beautiful person who is going to refine their beauty even more.

Let's do this!

Your Health

An examination of your physical health typically begins by creating a checklist of what you perceive as being wrong with you. Again, getting into this negative mindset is a downer, and it creates the feeling of swimming upstream against the current. Remember, I want you to swim downstream so this journey feels more free and effortless.

The way to do this is to think about aspects of your health that are perfect. Your body is a truly magnificent system composed of billions of cells and amazing intricate systems that you take for granted. If you know my story, you know that I have to manage symptoms related to multiple sclerosis (MS), which can be a big challenge.

However, as I manage my MS symptoms, I am also aware that my heart, kidneys, liver, brain cells, and bloodstream are doing a lot of amazing everyday routines that I take for granted. Put simply, if you're alive and breathing, a lot of good things are happening in your body!

If there are areas of your health that you would like to improve, start from the viewpoint that the cells in your body and your inner guidance system are eager to serve and to support you.

I'll give you an example from my life. When I was struggling with MS and the prescription drug train my doctors had put me on, I made a promise to myself that I would find a more holistic way to care for my body. The simple step of making this promise was incredibly significant. I didn't know exactly what this "more holistic way" would be, but I made a commitment to myself to start moving in that direction.

With this promise tucked tightly to my heart, an amazing thing began to happen. The stepping stones to a more holistic approach to mitigating my MS symptoms without drugs began to reveal themselves in ways I never would have imagined. My self-promise and these stepping stones led me to the healing power of expressive journaling, which has completely transformed my life.

I was a hero for myself by simply making a promise to ME. I didn't beat up on myself or force myself into some rigid program that required willpower and an inflexible devotion to something that didn't resonate with my inner guidance system.

Instead, I made a self-promise and trusted my heart and this empowered me to move downstream toward a wonderful solution that felt good. So, think about the issues in your tissues when it comes to your health. Think about an aspect of your health you'd like to change for the better. Now think about a promise you can make to YOU from a feeling of self-love that can begin a downstream journey on which you discover a solution that resonates with your soul.

Your Purpose and Fulfillment

We've all known people who appear to have it all. Good health, money, good looks, the house, the car, the clothes. And then we get to know these people and we often find they spend a lot of time alone in the comfort of their spacious backyards thinking, "Is this all there is?" Or, "I've got all the 'stuff' I ever wanted. Now what?"

The same questions are often asked by people I've known who live a minimalist lifestyle. No television, a small home, minimal monthly expenses, and very few material possessions. What you can conclude from this is that the amount of stuff we have or don't have has little to do with what we really want, which is to feel we are living our purpose. Living our purpose and doing what we believe we are meant to do in life lead to greater satisfaction and fulfillment.

Can you relate to these feelings? If you can, you have a head start toward defining your purpose and feeling fulfilled, because you are building a strong foundation of unconditional self-love that makes it much easier to design the life you WANT.

Also, being a hero for YOU can certainly include making a promise to yourself to form a clear vision of a life purpose that fills you with joy and happiness. Here are a few simple steps you can take to make such a promise from a place of unconditional self-love.

The first step you can take is to eliminate the word *should* from your process. Never start by asking yourself, "What should my purpose be?" This question immediately boxes you into a mental state in which you're trying to define a purpose for yourself that pleases others. You don't want to do this because this exercise is about making a promise that empowers you to be a hero for YOU, not someone else.

As I discussed in chapter two, the easiest way to get rid of the word *should* is simply to replace it with the word *could*.

Whereas the word *should* boxes you in, the word *could* releases you and empowers you to explore endless possibilities. When you ask yourself, "What could my purpose be?", your inner guidance system will fill you with a list of ideas you can write in your journal as they come to you.

As you examine your list of options you can then ask yourself the magical question, "What do I WANT my purpose to be?" At this point, promise yourself that you'll allow your heart to provide you with your answer. Don't immediately jump into your head and think too hard as you try to "figure out" what you want your purpose to be.

Remember, you don't make your best decisions—you FEEL them.

So get out of your head and allow what you truly want your purpose to be to flow into your heart. If you do, you'll FEEL your self-mission through a strong sense of inner knowing. You won't really have to think about it, it will just come to you.

The answer may take a few days to fill your being, but it will. It may come to you while you're out on a hike, or while taking a shower, while doing some yard work, or in some other moment when you least expect it. But it WILL come to you, and when it does you'll be overcome by a definite sense of certainty.

Making a promise to go through this basic exercise is a simple but glorious way to be a hero for YOU!

Your Relationships

The most wide-ranging and expansive area of your life involves the relationships you have with other people. More than any other aspect of your life, if you mapped out all the relationships you have it would probably resemble a massive spider web. This is because we have personal relationships with an array of people that includes our:

- Spouse/partner/significant other
- Children
- Parents
- Siblings
- Friends
- Relatives
- Neighbors
- Co-workers
- Industry colleagues
- And the list goes on

Making this spider web even more complex is that the role we play as a person usually changes depending on with whom we are interacting. For example, how you "act" while interacting with your children is probably much different than how you act when you're engaging with industry colleagues.

As you consider the relationships in your life, think of a promise you can make to YOU that will make one (or more) of these relationships more satisfying and fulfilling.

Here is an example of how such a promise might look: Make a promise to YOU that you're going to make your relationship with your spouse more important than your relationship with your children. You can even take this a step further and promise yourself that your relationship with YOU should be priority number one, your relationship with your spouse should be number two, and your relationship with your children should be priority number three.

To many parents, this may sound completely out of order and even a bit terrifying given your number one priority as a parent is to care for your children. However, I know people who've made a promise like this to themselves and their reason for making it sounded like this: "If I promise to love myself first I'll be in a much stronger position to love my spouse and nurture our relationship. If my relationship with ME and my relationship with my spouse is strong, I'll be in a much more positive place from which I can be the best version of me as a parent, which will greatly benefit my children."

This is just one example of the many types of promises you can make to yourself as you consider the numerous relationships in your life. Perhaps you can consider the example I've given you, and think about a promise you can make to yourself regarding a relationship in your life that centers around showing yourself unconditional love and being a hero for YOU.

Your Wealth

It's all about the money, honey. Or is it?

The subject of money is a hot-button issue in the tissues that ignites a wide range of feelings and beliefs in different people. Some still believe that money is the root of all evil.

Others believe the accumulation of wealth is a splendid pursuit because having more money gives you the ability to help more people.

Maybe you subscribe to one of these two positions, or maybe your attitudes and beliefs about money fall somewhere in between. No matter where your thoughts about money lie, it's hard to argue that wealth creation isn't the ultimate touchy subject for this reason:

When you think about the list of touchy subjects in our culture, money is the one you absolutely cannot avoid. Think about it. Sex is a touchy subject. But you can abstain from sex or put it on the back-burner for a while if you choose. Religion is a touchy subject. But it's rather easy to avoid religion if you choose to. Politics is another touchy subject. But you don't have to watch the news every night if you don't want to, and you can even choose not to vote. If people try to engage you in a conversation about your political beliefs, you can simply tell them it's none of their business and then avoid them in the future.

Although there is a list of touchy subjects in our culture, most of them are easy to avoid and ignore if you really want to.

Money, on the other hand, is different.

You don't have to talk to people about money if you don't want to, but you certainly can't avoid it and you definitely have to think about it. Why? Because unlike sex, religion, and politics, you need to make money, manage money, spend money, and make more money. This is something living in modern society demands from you.

This means you have no choice but to become really clear about your feelings as they pertain to money and wealth. Now, I want to be clear that how you feel about money and wealth is up to you. Again, as you settle into YOUR thoughts and beliefs about money you want to feel as though you're swimming downstream with the current.

Here is an example of one kind of promise you can make to be a hero for you when it comes to the subject of money.

Say, for example, you'd like to make more money but you have a deep-seated belief that if you do it will deprive less fortunate people of having what they need to meet their basic financial needs. In such a case, your self-promise may look like this.

"I promise to be a hero for ME by developing a new belief that says 'wealth is like health.' Just as my reaching a higher level of physical health doesn't deprive anyone else of being healthy, my accumulating wealth doesn't deprive anyone else of being wealthy, because just like the creation of good health, the creation of wealth is available to everyone. Just like good health, wealth is not a pie with only so many slices to go around. Rather, the ability for everyone to create financial wealth is unlimited, just like the ability to create good health is unlimited. Plus, the more wealth I create, the more people and causes I can support."

This is but one example of many promises you can make to be a hero for YOU when it comes to money. When you make such a promise and form a belief and a strong desire that you WANT to see this promise come to fruition, it's only a matter of time before stepping stones will begin to appear before you that lead you down your chosen path.

No matter what your feelings about money and wealth may be, be a hero for you by making a promise that will amplify these feelings and turn them into your financial reality.

Your Journaling Power Prompt

Grab your journal and think about each of the areas of your life of which we just took a quick glance. Consider other areas we didn't cover as well. Now pick just ONE of these areas. Maybe for you it's your health, or perhaps it's building wealth through your business. It's up to you because it's YOUR life.

I'm asking you to pick just one area because I want you to think BIG. Plus, when you're thinking BIG it's so much easier to focus on ONE main thing. So choose one area of your life, and be a hero for YOU by making ONE big promise to yourself.

Again, make it a promise that gives you a sense of swimming downstream with the current. For example, if you want to transform your health by losing some weight, don't make the mistake we've all made by saying, "Starting Monday, I'm going to go on a trendy new diet that is 100% different than what I eat currently."

This approach never works because it makes you feel like you're swimming upstream against the current, which always tires you out and makes you give up.

However, what if you made a promise that, starting Monday, you were going to explore some healthy changes you could make to your daily eating plan that you could gradually implement over the next six to eight weeks. Afterall, what's six to eight weeks when you're going to be eating every day for the rest of your life? Plus, this is a heroic promise to yourself that will make you feel like you're moving downstream with the current.

This is but one example of a promise you can make to be your own hero. What promise do you want to make to YOU? Choose one area of your life and make your promise. I'm only asking you to choose one area and to make one promise. So go BIG, and be bold and heroic.

Chapter 11

Love the Journey Because You Never Really Get "There"

If you've made it this far you're on a roll, and you no doubt have developed a passion for showering yourself with unconditional love. Good for you!

Last chapter, we explored promises you can make to yourself so that you can be a hero for YOU. The promises you chose to make to you might be similar or different to the promise your fellow **Journaling Power** revolutionaries may have made to themselves.

However, in this chapter I want to focus on a more universal promise I'd like to see you make to yourself. That promise is to love yourself through every moment of every journey on which you embark in life.

Here is why this is so important.

You no doubt have heard the expression that the journey is more important than the destination. The sentiment being that if you don't feel joy and happiness during your journey, you're fooling yourself if you believe you'll suddenly feel joy and happiness when you arrive there, wherever "there" may be.

I'm going to take this thought and expand on it even more by saying that you absolutely MUST enjoy the journey because that's all you have in life. Put bluntly, it's been my experience that you never really reach your destination or your "there." Even when you believe you do, you only enjoy it for a fleeting moment until you begin thinking about your next destination, and then another journey begins.

Here's what I mean.

You go on a journey in search of a higher-paying job. You get the job and you're excited! You've arrived at your destination. You're "there." And then a few short days later, that excitement is quickly replaced by the anxiety and nervousness that comes with starting a new job and all of the responsibilities that come with it.

You go on a journey of working long, hard hours in the months leading up to a one-week vacation. When you leave work on the Friday before your vacation begins, you're ecstatic! However, within a day your excitement is replaced with the stress that comes with packing, getting to the airport, getting through security, dealing with flight delays, and the hustle and grind that go with "vacationing." Then the next thing you know, you're back at home and it's time to go back to work.

You go on a journey in search of a new lover or partner. This journey can certainly be stressful and filled with ups and downs, but you grind and persist. And then, you meet someone. Hooray! You're in a state of euphoric bliss! However, then you begin to miss the complete freedom you had when you were single. And, perhaps you begin to resent all of the changes you're being asked to make to accommodate your lover's expectations of you. Or, perhaps you just slowly settle into a new life routine that begins to repeat itself peacefully week after week, month after month.

I certainly don't use these examples to be a downer! My point is simply that we tend to spend the overwhelming majority of our time on our journeys, while spending very little time at our destinations, whether they are physical or mental. When we do arrive at our destinations, we typically enjoy the sensation for a bit before we start thinking about our next destination and the journey we must take to get "there."

This is why it is so critical that you enjoy your journey. What you think of as your destination or your "there" really is an illusion. What you think of as your destination is actually just another step in your journey.

So there really is no "there." All you have is your journey, which is why you must enjoy every moment and every step of it. And, the only moment you can really enjoy is the one you have right NOW.

That's because when it really comes down to it, all you have is now. And, unless you discover how to feel better now, you won't feel better when the new lover arrives or when the new job arrives. Sure, you'll feel a sudden surge of excitement, but it will dissipate in due time. However, what you always have is the steps you're taking on your journey right now, so it's essential you enjoy the moment right now.

Here is some insight into why this is so.

Shiny Object Syndrome

If you've been involved in business, especially an online business, you're probably familiar with the term, "shiny object syndrome." This syndrome typically occurs when an online entrepreneur wants to do something new, like develop an online program.

Rather than simply sit down and develop the program, an entrepreneur may decide to buy an online program that teaches them how to create an online program. The entrepreneur gets excited about the program, gets three quarters of the way through it ...gets a little bored with the program ... and then buys a different online program that teaches them how to create an online program.

In this case, the shiny object is the online program that's going to teach the entrepreneur how to create online programs. Once the shine diminishes from the online program, the entrepreneur ignores it and then moves on to another online training program, or shiny new object.

So, what does the shiny object syndrome have to do with enjoying your journey because you never really get "there?" It's simple. The "destinations" you put in your mind, like finding the new lover, getting the new job, or buying the new car, are all examples of shiny objects. When we acquire such shiny objects we get really excited and experience a nice *dopamine rush*. Ok, I can hear you asking, "What the heck's a dopamine rush?"

In really simple terms, dopamine is known as a feel-good neurotransmitter that plays a huge role in feeling excitement and pleasure. Your brain releases it when you eat good-tasting foods that you crave, when you make love, and when you get excited about buying a shiny online program that teaches you how to make online programs.

In a nutshell, when you do something or achieve something that makes you feel excitement and pleasure, you're having a dopamine rush. However, as you know from your life experiences, a dopamine rush is rather fleeting and doesn't last very long.

A perfect example of this is the absolute excitement you felt as a kid when you received new toys on your birthday. Remember how ecstatic and excited you felt as you unwrapped your presents and held a new toy in your hands? This was a dopamine rush!

But then what happened? Well, if you were like a lot of kids, within a month or two that dopamine rush had long since subsided and your new toy (shiny object) became old news and became yet another toy that got shoved under your bed to collect dust.

You may have seen children in your life go through this dopamine rush cycle without realizing that you and I go through a grown-up version of this as adults. Here are a few examples:

- The dopamine rush you feel when you land a better job … and then it wears off and you settle into a new daily routine.
- The dopamine rush you feel when you buy a new car … and then it gets dirty and you need to wash it and change the oil, etc.
- The dopamine rush you feel when you buy new clothes … and then they go out of style and are put in the corner of your closet to collect dust.

The fact is, you spend a lot of your life in search of the next dopamine rush that you'll feel when you arrive at your new destination, or your next "there."

Knowing that the dopamine rush you feel when you reach a "destination" or achieve a goal won't last very long is why you have to enjoy your moment-by-moment journey in life.

You Discard What You Once Embraced

Further proof of this point is exemplified by how you discard things, and even people, that once got you so excited. Consider the "spring cleaning" you probably do in your home from time to time. Clothes that excited you when you bought them are pulled from the corner of your closet and put into plastic bags that you give to charity. Gadgets, electronics, appliances, and other things that were once "shiny objects" are casually tossed into the trash or taken to the recycling center when they're deemed old and outdated.

A lover that you once couldn't get off of your mind may now be someone you haven't spoken to in years. The group of friends that you couldn't wait to spend every weekend with once upon a time may now just be profiles on Facebook that you occasionally see in your newsfeed.

If your life is like mine or the lives of a lot of people I know, you tend to journey from one dopamine rush to the next. Some of these "rushes" are big, like buying a new car or landing a new job, and some are little, like when you buy a new gadget for your kitchen that you will one day throw out. But what all of our dopamine rush moments have in common is that they are temporary.

Now don't get me wrong: dopamine-driven celebrations are an exhilarating and special part of life. They bring you great pleasure and fulfillment. It's just important that you and

I realize every dopamine-driven rush of excitement you feel over reaching a destination eventually subsides.

In short, you and I tend to embrace things, people, and moments much like we embrace other shiny objects. We pursue them, get them, enjoy them, and eventually discard them as we mentally cycle from excitement to disinterest.

This is perfectly normal as you move through life. The key point here is that you don't need to wait until you arrive at your various destinations in life to feel excitement and pleasure. This is an especially important point of view to hold when you realize that the overwhelming majority of your time in life is the time you spend on journeys that eventually lead you to new destinations and the attainment of shiny objects.

Knowing this is the case is all the reason you need to discover ways to make every moment of your life's journeys as delicious and joyful as possible. This is much easier to do when you absolutely love yourself.

Your Destination is NOW

When you love yourself, every day can be a dopamine rush day! It's become cliche to say that all you really have is NOW, but it really is true. You can never relive the past, and tomorrow never comes because every day is *today*. Or as John Lennon once said, "Life is what happens to you while you're busy making other plans."

Now, I realize you can't just purely live for the moment and run off to San Francisco and improvise your own little Summer of Love (unless you really WANT to!). You do have to make plans, and you do have to execute daily routines that keep you moving forward and productive. You have bills to pay, goals to achieve, people to care for, pets to look after, and colleagues and co-workers who depend on you.

What I just described to you is the daily journey on which you embark in between the attainment of shiny objects and your arrival at new destinations. Well, I'm here to tell you that every moment of your daily journey can feel like you've arrived at a glorious new destination. All you have to do is tell yourself that your next destination is NOW.

All you have is NOW. Your life is never going to get better until you make it better right now. If it's Tuesday, life won't get better on the weekend unless you can find a way to make it better right now. You're not going to attract that new lover who makes you feel excited two months from now, unless you discover how to smother yourself with unconditional love and excite yourself right now.

The way to do this is to make your next "destination" NOW. I've got some great ideas about how you can do this coming up in Chapter 12, but you can start building some momentum right NOW by grabbing your pen and your journal.

Your Journaling Power Prompt

When you have a destination in mind it can be easy to slide into a belief that the journey you must take to get "there" will be arduous and void of joy. It's also easy to tell yourself that you're willing to accept this because you'll feel happy and have a big dopamine rush at the end when you finally get "there."

However, there is no need to delay joy and happiness in your life until you get there, wherever there might be for you. Remember, that "new car smell" only lasts so long, and then you quickly set your sights on another destination. The thrill of finally taking that vacation quickly fades when you get back home and slide back into your daily routines.

The vast majority of your life is spent being on the journey, not arriving at a destination. So it's vital your journeys be joyful and fulfilling. Here is a journaling prompt that will help you achieve this.

Grab your pen and your journal, and write down the words:

"I am so grateful now that ..."

Conclude this statement by writing about a "destination" you have in mind as if you're already there. If your destination is a new job or starting your own business, write about it as if it's in your life NOW. Don't write about it as if it's a destination that is far off in the distance. Give gratitude for the fact that you're already there.

For example, you may write, "I am so grateful now that I run my own business and have the freedom to work at home and set my own schedule."

Describe what this looks like and how it feels. Detail the positive emotions stirring within you. Write about how much more energized and enthusiastic you feel. Write about how you're going to act now that you have either mentally or physically arrived where you want to be.

When you journal in such an affirmative way, you can't help but feel fantastic right NOW, which is all you really have.

Remember, your life isn't when the new job gets here, it isn't when the new lover arrives, and it isn't when those pesky five extra pounds finally disappear. Your life is NOW. So you have to feel happy NOW, because NOW is all you really have.

If you write about where you want to get to as if you're already there, you will no doubt get there much faster, and you'll feel extraordinary throughout the journey.

Chapter 12

Transform Your Life By Asking the Right Questions

In chapter eleven, I focused on the importance of enjoying your NOW because there really is no long-lasting "there" or "destination" at which you're going to arrive and experience a continued state of euphoria. Shiny objects only stay shiny for so long, and the dopamine rush we all crave is always short lived.

However, what you can count on is that your life is continuing to unfold before you at a steady and predictable pace, day in and day out. It is this steady unfolding that forms 99% of your life, which is why it's essential that you do what it takes to make yourself feel good now.

You and I also established in chapter eleven that you can't have an unhappy journey and expect to suddenly get happy when you achieve a goal, find a new job, or meet a new lover. Your life is a continuous journey, so feeling good right now means everything.

So, make up your mind and commit to the principle that nothing is more important than how you feel right now. You have to start feeling great at some point, so it might as well be right now. Put simply, your destination needs to be NOW.

This chapter is all about asking yourself questions, and the question on your mind right now might be, "I'm with you, Mari, but how do I always make myself feel better NOW?"

If this is what's on your mind, you're off to a great start because you're asking a wonderful question.

One of the ways you've probably heard you can put yourself in a good-feeling state is to develop positive affirmations and repeat them to yourself over and over as you maneuver your way through your daily life.

Don't get me wrong, I think affirmations are wonderful, especially when you're meditating or taking a quiet walk in nature. However, affirmations can be difficult to repeat and keep in the forefront of your mind as you're bobbing and weaving your way through your day.

On the other hand, asking yourself the right questions is an incredible tool you can use every moment of your life to keep yourself in a positive state of self-love in which you feel like you're in the flow and moving downstream. Asking questions is a super-effective way to manage your mental state right now for this simple reason ...

... You're Constantly Asking Yourself Questions

You and I spend a great big, giant chunk of our daily lives caught up in self-talk chatter that we continually bounce around our minds. This revelation is no surprise to you because we're all aware we do this. And of course we thank our lucky stars that no one else can hear our self-chatter!

However, what you may not be aware of is how much of your mental self-chatter revolves around asking yourself questions:

- How do I do this?
- How do I get there?

- Why doesn't this work anymore?
- What did he really mean by that?
- How come she hasn't responded to my text?
- Why does she always have to act that way?
- Does this guy realize how obnoxious he is?
- Where the hell are my car keys?
- When's a good time to workout?
- Do I have enough food in the fridge?
- Why does the dog keep itching himself?
- Why can't I shut off the noise in my head?
- How the heck am I going to find time to do that?

The list goes on and on and on. You are constantly asking yourself questions. Tons of them in fact!

Make Your Destination NOW By Asking Empowering Questions

It may feel a little strange when you take the time to realize how many questions you ask yourself during the day. However, I'm going to ask that you use this realization as an excuse to shower yourself with love. Why? Because asking yourself the RIGHT questions throughout the day can be an incredibly empowering and a fantastic way to make NOW your destination.

The reason why asking yourself the right questions is so empowering is because the questions you ask yourself tend to immediately pop you into a specific frame of mind whether you realize it or not. And that frame of mind can be debilitating or transformative, depending on the questions you ask.

For example, let's pretend you have a friend named Dave who has held a "safe and steady" job for 10 years. However, the company for which Dave works hits a rough patch and decides it must reorganize it's workforce, and Dave is laid off and loses his job in the reshuffle.

After absorbing the shock from this sudden jolt, Dave finds himself sitting on his couch a few days later with a series of questions racing through his mind. This list of questions Dave asks himself could look like this:

- Why me? Why did this have to happen to me?
- How will I ever be able to find another good job? Who'll want to hire me?
- What am I going to do about money? Will I run out? How can I possibly make ends meet?

However, the list of questions running around Dave's mind could also look like this:

- Is losing this job a sign that I was meant to do bigger things in life?
- Could this be the perfect time to start the consulting business I've been dreaming about?
- What's good about this situation? What's the deeper message I can leverage to come back bigger, wiser, and better than ever?

Now ask yourself this: Which set of questions is going to energize Dave and put him in a more powerful frame of mind where he is able to love himself unconditionally and take inspired actions that improve his life? Which set of questions is going to make Dave feel better NOW?

I think you'll agree: the second set of questions is going to better serve Dave by putting him in a frame of mind in which he decides he can manifest a more fulfilling life. The second set of questions is going to affect his posture, his breathing, and every single cell in his body for the better.

There's no question about it. Questions are powerful, and you are constantly asking yourself questions throughout the day. So make them good ones! Questions are a simple but tremendous way to make the step you're taking right NOW in your journey much more positive.

In a nutshell, a great way to make your destination of NOW a great one is to ask yourself empowering questions. This is so much easier, and even more natural, than repeating affirmations hundreds of times throughout your day.

Asking life-affirming questions at any given moment is a powerful tool you can leverage to fuel yourself with positive energy and unconditional love right NOW. Let's take a closer look at how you can tap into the power of questions in various areas of your life.

Health

Holistic practitioners and doctors who practice functional medicine are in wide agreement that your thoughts and state of mind have a direct effect on every cell in your body and thus, your overall health. So it's a great idea to create a list of questions about your health that will excite your mind, body, and spirit. Here are some examples:

- What am I most grateful for today in regards
  to my health?
- What aspect of my physical body do I most admire?
- What can I do to relax and calm my body right now?
- What one simple thing can I do today to make
  sure I eat healthy?
- What aspect of my health seems always to flow
  with ease and without dis-ease?

This is just a quick sampling of empowering questions you can ask yourself about your health each day. Take the ball and run with it from here!

Relationships

Newsflash: The quality of your relationships has a tremendous impact on the quality of every aspect of your life. From co-workers, to kids, to spouses, to lovers, to friends, your relationships can fill you with euphoria and glee, and they can also make you want to scream at the top of your lungs as you run off into the mountains never to be seen again.

Given the highs and lows you experience in your various relationships, having a strong set of questions you can turn to in a pinch is a must. Here are some sample questions that may come in handy when you run into a rough patch with your significant other:

- What's the one positive thing I can always rely
  on with my partner every day?
- What personality trait do I most admire about
  my partner?

- What was the magic spark that initially attracted
  me to my partner?
- What can I do to better listen to my partner's concerns?
- What simple thing can I do to better communicate
  my feelings to my partner?

You have a lot of relationships in your life. Perhaps you can pick one that is a little bumpy right now and shape a list of positive questions around it.

Career

So much of our self-esteem and identity is tied to our careers. People who lose their jobs often report that the loss of identity they feel is more of a body blow than their loss of income. Whether you work for someone or whether you're self-employed, how you view yourself is often shaped by how you see yourself through the prism of your career.

Since so much of your life is spent working to "bring home the bacon" and "make a name for yourself," it's vital that you have a list of questions you can ask yourself so that NOW feels like a vibrant moment as you journey through your career. Here are some sample questions that may jumpstart your work day:

- How can I provide assistance and value to
  others today?
- How can I make people feel good about
  interacting with me today?
- How can I improve my primary skill by
  just one percent today?

- What can I do to make my least enjoyable task today a little humorous?
- How would I walk, talk, and breathe if all of my business goals for the next five years have already been achieved?

There are a slew of uplifting questions you can ask yourself to make your work day more satisfying. Have some fun and see how many you can add to this list.

Financial Abundance

They say "money makes the world" go around. I'm not sure if this is true (I vote for love), but I do know that thinking about money can certainly make your head feel like it's spinning a lot faster. The truth is, people have a wide range of feelings and beliefs they've attached to money, and you no doubt have your own set of beliefs and values.

However, it's been my experience that most people with whom I interact would appreciate having more money. Regardless of how you feel about the importance of money, there is no denying that having enough of it is essential to living a fulfilling life in our culture. With this in mind, here are some sample questions that can put you in a frame of mind for attracting and making more money:

- If I could blow $1,000 today, how would I spend it?
- Where would I live and what would I do if money wasn't a barrier?
- What successful person's habits can I model to increase my wealth?

- What one alteration to my daily routine can I make to increase my earning potential?
- What charities will I give money to when I double or triple my income?
- How would I walk, talk, and feel if I had 10 million dollars in my checking account?
- How do I feel knowing that wealth, like health, is something everyone can have?

There are a lot of questions you can design to make you feel great about money, and there is a long list of questions you can create to make you feel bad or mad about money. The choice is yours.

Unconditional Self-Love

If you've made it to chapter 12 of this book, I have every reason to believe you understand how crucial it is to shower yourself with unconditional love. Yet, I also understand that you and I have our moments when it's a challenge to love ourselves as much as we should.

In fact, it can be a challenge at times to believe you're worthy of receiving unconditional self-love from YOU every minute of every day. But you are! Absolutely, positively you are! Here are some sample questions you can reflect on at any given moment to make sure your NOW is awash in self-love and appreciation:

- What is the one wonderful thing about me I'd never want to change?

- What talent do I have that I am so very proud of?
- What have I done to bring value to somebody's life this week?
- What incredibly nice thing would my pet say about me if she could talk?
- What goals have I set in my life that I have followed through on and achieved?
- What have I done in the last three days that I should celebrate?
- What can I do to pamper myself today?

When you love yourself without conditions, this is a list of questions you should be able to add to rapidly with a great big grin on your face!

Spoiler alert: for your journaling prompt, I'm going to ask you to create your own list of questions for various areas of your life. However, as part of this exercise I also invite you to consider the list of questions I just provided to you as a warm up for your journaling prompt.

I'm certain that if you re-examine the questions above throughout your day you'll find yourself looking at YOU from a refreshing new perspective. I think you'll be further convinced of the power questions play in altering your state of mind, your posture, and the way you carry yourself.

Now, on to your journaling prompt!

Your Journaling Power Prompt

Given the ground I just covered, this journaling prompt is going to be fun and uplifting. I've broken it down into two parts.

Part 1

Grab your journal and focus on an area of your life covered in this chapter, and then create 10 self-empowering questions pertaining to that area that will immediately put you in a positive and energized state of self-love.

This is a very simple and straightforward journaling prompt, so I suggest that over time you do this 10-questions exercise for every area of your life. It will be fun!

Part 2

After you've put together a few lists of 10 energizing questions that pertain to various areas of your life, make an "all-star" list of top 10 questions you can keep nearby at all times. These 10 questions can touch on various aspects of your life.

The goal here is to assemble a group of 10 "go-to" questions you can read each morning and throughout the day, knowing they're going to pick you up and put you in a positive mental state. Here are some examples of the kind of questions you can consider for your top-10 list:

- What can I do today to advance myself a little closer to my goal?
- Where can I find 30 minutes today to have fun and play like a kid and nurture my inner child?

- What personal characteristic do I have that I absolutely love but often take for granted?
- What lesson can I learn today to gain a little more wisdom than I had yesterday?
- What little thing can I do today that will give me a good reason to celebrate tonight?

These are just sample questions. Hopefully they'll provide you with a springboard for crafting your own list of self-empowering questions that make you feel as though you're flowing downstream in a river of unconditional self-love.

Really follow through on this exercise, and perhaps after a week or so you can ask yourself this important question: Is the quality of my questions beginning to have a positive impact on how I feel right NOW?

I strongly believe the answer to this question will be, "Yes!" If it is, know that you can further improve your state of mind at any given moment by revising and sharpening your questions so they make you feel even better!

Chapter 13

Marry Yourself

Congratulations! You've made it to chapter 13, which means you are a bonafide unconditional self-love rock star! The fact that you've made it this far tells me you're in it to win it. So let's take it all the way.

You've built a lot of love-yourself momentum up to this point, and I intend to guide you to the top of self-love mountain. If you stick with me, I promise you the view from the summit will be spectacular!

In honor of the incredible progress you've made since you began reading this book, I have a special surprise for you in this chapter. This is going to be fun for me, because it gives me a chance to play "Mari the Matchmaker." Here's the surprise:

If you're happily married, I have a wonderful chance for you to be happily married twice. If you're single, man I have found the absolute perfect companion for you.

Whether you're already married to a partner or a single person in the market for love, the perfect person I have found for you to marry is YOU! I mean, after all: if you're going to put in all this effort to love yourself unconditionally, you may as well go all the way with it and marry yourself.

Now, I realize the concept of marrying yourself may sound lighthearted and fun, but it is actually a very self-empowering and healthy thing to do. Here's why.

Remember Our Flight Attendant Story?

Earlier I reminded you of the instructions airline flight attendants give you just before your plane departs: In the event of a loss in cabin pressure a yellow mask will pop down through which you can breathe. Make sure your mask is secure and you're breathing freely before you attempt to help others with their masks.

These instructions make perfect sense of course, because if your mask isn't secure you'll black out and be unable to help others. Before you can be a hero for others you have to be a hero for yourself. Before you can help others strengthen their personal foundation, you have to solidify your own. Before you can be a great partner for someone else, you have to be a great partner for yourself. Before you can be devoted to someone else with all of your heart, you must first be devoted to YOU.

The one person you have been with your entire life is the one person you ALWAYS will be with, and that's YOU. So it makes perfect sense to love yourself and to marry yourself.

Now, before we get to the inspiring little ceremony in which you get to marry yourself, I'm going to ask you to make some promises and commitments that you vow to never break.

These are commitments and vows that society has taught us to make to others instead of ourselves, but it is absolutely essential that you make them to yourself first. Putting YOU first will give you the strong foundation you need to make these promises to others.

Be Loyal to Yourself

Throughout your life, you've heard a number of people from various spiritual, cultural, and political points of view tell you where your loyalties should lie, and in what order they should lie. For example, you've heard your loyalties should be to God, family, and country. You may have also heard they should be to country, family, and the corporation for whom you work. I know that in my life I've heard a dozen or more variations of what the proper "order of loyalty" should be. You probably have too.

However, you've probably never heard any righteous authority figure say that your first loyalty should be to YOU. This is because in most Western cultures it is considered "selfish" to put yourself first ahead of God, family, and country. Well, my question to you is this: What good are you to God, your family, or your country if you're a mess inside? Heck, what good are you to your dog or your cat if you're a mess inside?

The truth is, and so what if this sounds selfish, your first loyalty has to be to YOU. Because when you love yourself and feel great about yourself, you can be of much greater service to God (Spirit, Him/Her The Infinite One), family, your community, your country, and your pets.

Nurture Yourself

How many times in your life have you heard this line directed at certain people, especially women: "She was so selfless that she always put taking care of others ahead of taking care of herself."

You've probably heard this said about people many times throughout your life, and it's usually intended to be a compliment or a badge of honor of some kind. But when do you typically hear this being said about someone? After they have died, of course ... because they were too busy taking care of others to nurture themselves.

Don't get me wrong, being selfless and of service to others is noble and an admirable personal characteristic. But again, you can nurture others with more compassion and empathy if you've taken the time to solidify your personal foundation by nurturing YOU first.

So please promise me that you'll find time each day to be good to yourself. The people you love most in life will benefit from simple acts of self-love you direct to YOU.

Encourage Yourself

Promise me that part of marrying yourself will include encouraging yourself each and every day. There are probably moments in your life when you look back on your childhood and think thoughts along the lines of, "Why didn't my father encourage me more?" "Why didn't my mother tell me to think big and shoot for the stars?" "Why didn't anybody tell me that I was smart and had unlimited potential to achieve anything I wanted?"

None of us received all of the encouragement we wish we would have received as a kid. However, there is nothing stopping you from giving yourself the encouragement NOW that you wish you would have received years ago.

In fact, (*journaling prompt spoiler alert*) every day of your life you can play the role of your own parent and give yourself all the love and encouragement you wish you would have received growing up. An important part of loving yourself and committing to yourself unconditionally is encouraging yourself each and every day.

So what if your mother or father didn't tell you that you are smart, beautiful, and capable of achieving anything to which you set your mind? Give yourself this encouragement right NOW. Later on today, do it again! Encouraging yourself throughout every day of your life is perfectly healthy, and doing so will make you feel fantastic.

Forgive Yourself

Nobody is perfect. Not you, not me, and not anybody else who pretends to be. We all have flaws and we all have regrets. That's just part of the human experience. So before you take the big leap and marry yourself, commit to forgiving yourself for choices in the past that were less than your best.

I believe the most important aspect of self-forgiveness is letting go. Learn the lessons from your regrets and move forward. You cannot go back in time and undo anything, but you certainly can learn lessons from your past and apply them to what you're doing NOW.

Unless you're able to collect monthly payments from bad decisions that haunt you and occupy space inside your head, you may as well evict them. Just let them go and tell them to get lost. Again, no one is perfect. Everybody has a laundry list of bad choices they wish they could go back in time and turn into smart choices. But you can't.

What you can do is love yourself enough to let go and forgive yourself, and use the lessons you've learned from your mistakes as a springboard for growth.

Allow Yourself to Play Like a Kid

This is a fun promise to make. There is no doubt that your inner child travels along with you everywhere you go. After all, you've always been YOU. Whether you're eight years old, 19 years old, 35 years old, or 52 years old, your inner child has always been inside that body of yours.

And what did you enjoy doing most when you were eight or nine years old? You enjoyed playing like a child because you were a child. Well, that child still lives within you so please promise me that you'll always find time to play like a kid. Why? Because it's fun!

Fellow journaling revolutionary, Casey Demchak, tells me that he loves putting long hours into his copywriting business. But he also says his favorite part of the day is when he spends an hour as if he was still a seven-year-old boy: walking his dog and playing with him. And his dog, of course, absolutely loves this time of day!

What did you love to do when you were a child as a playful activity? Sports? Drawing? Board games? Building models? Designing doll houses? Recapture the magic of your childhood by doing something you loved doing as a kid, and keep doing it as an adult. You don't even have to tell anyone about it. Just promise me, and promise YOU, that you'll always give yourself permission to make time to play like a kid.

Do this, and I guarantee you it will put a wonderful grin across your face.

Realize Others Will Love You as You Love Yourself

What if you knew for certain that the extent to which others love you is an exact match to the extent to which you love yourself? Is this formula absolutely true? I have no scientific evidence to confirm it, but I will always believe it.

I believe it, because I'm certain that like energy attracts like energy. When you put out a certain vibration it tends to attract back to you. For this reason, I'm convinced that the love you attract from others equals the love you feel for yourself.

When you feel confident, you tend to inspire people to feel confident in you. When you express doubts in your ability to do a particular task, you're unlikely to draw people to you who believe you can do it.

As automotive legend Henry Ford once said, "Whether you think you can, or think you can't -- you're right." You've also no doubt heard the expressions "Misery loves company," "When you go looking for trouble, trouble always finds you," or, "What goes around comes around."

We have numerous ways in our culture of expressing the belief that the vibration we put out to the Universe determines what comes back to us. If you believe this principle to any extent, then you must believe that the degree to which you love yourself plays a powerful role in the level of love that comes back to you from others.

And we all want a river of love to flow back to us, so promise me as you marry yourself you'll shower yourself with daily buckets of unconditional self-love. Then you can bask in the glory of having it come back to you!

Marry Yourself

It doesn't have to be an elaborate ceremony, and there's no need to blow a lot of money on the occasion. You can do it while you're meditating, soaking in a warm bath, going for a hike in nature, or while you're standing before a full-length mirror. But go ahead and marry yourself.

Tell everyone you know, or keep it to yourself. But go ahead and make an unbreakable lifetime commitment to YOU. Make a vow and promise to cherish yourself, to honor yourself, to forgive yourself, to protect yourself, and to always love yourself.

Write your wedding vows and read them aloud. Give yourself a few days off to celebrate the occasion. You will always be YOU and you will always be with YOU, so commit from the bottom of your heart to love yourself without conditions and to make your forever with YOU a fantastic experience!

As a simple little wedding gift, I invite you to use one of my favorite hashtags when you and I interact online.

#MarryYourself!

Your Journaling Power Prompt

This journaling prompt can be magical as you venture through your joyous journey of unconditional self-love. It can be magical for this reason. It gives you the chance to be your own parent and say to yourself all of the things you wish your parents would have said to you.

I don't know your personal background. You may have had a wonderful relationship with your parents, and they may have been fountains of love and inspiration for you. Or, you may have had mentally- abusive parents who had little in the way of positive things to say to you. Or, your relationship with your parents may have fallen somewhere in between the utopia and living nightmares I just outlined.

I can't possibly know your specific situation, but I do know that you probably have a laundry list of things you wish your parents would have said to you. Well, now is your chance to step back in time, be your own parent, and say all the things to a younger you that you wish you would have heard from your mom and dad.

I really urge you to get into this journaling prompt because it can make you feel fantastic! So grab your pen and your journal and do it!

First, form a vision of you in your mind as a young 10-year-old kid who has hopes, dreams, aspirations, questions about the world, and talents you don't fully appreciate yet.

Now step aside in this vision and view yourself standing a few feet away, looking at you as a 10-year-old child. Become your own parent and write down everything you would say to this precious 10-year old child if it was your intent to encourage them to pursue their dreams, achieve everything they want in their life, and love themselves.

Don't hold back. This 10-year-old child loves you, admires, looks up to you, and counts on you for hope, inspiration and guidance. What would you say to this 10-year-old YOU? Write it all down and don't hold back. Love this child, encourage this child, and fill this child with confidence, joy, determination, and certainty. Use your words to love this child with all your heart.

Pour your heart and soul into this exercise, and then read everything you've written out loud. And then realize this 10-year-old child is still living within you and still craves your love, encouragement, and devotion.

Chapter 14

Conclusion: What's YOUR Self-Love Mindset Medicine Mission?

Through the first 13 chapters of this book, you've done an amazing job of building your unconditional self-love momentum muscle. How do I know this? Simple. You wouldn't be reading this if you had given up prior to this point.

The fact that you're still with me says that you've become a full-fledged unconditional self-love revolutionary. You've stuck with it, you've shown a tremendous level of dedication to YOU, and you've demonstrated you're committed to a lifetime journey of unconditional self-love. You should be extremely proud of yourself!

As we wind things down, I am going to ask you to promise yourself that you'll commit to a strong finish. Rather than coasting your way to the end of this journey, I am going to ask that you catch your second wind and prepare to throw things into an even higher gear.

Think of this as the final hundred yards of a long-distance race. This is where you summon up every ounce of energy within you so you can kick things up one more notch and bust past the finish line in a blaze of glory.

Given that you're still with me, I imagine that, like me, you view the mindset medicine process of fueling your soul with unconditional self-love as a magical experience. It's similar to unwrapping a gift. It excites and energizes you as you're doing it. And when you finish unwrapping a gift, you get to hold it in your hand and ask yourself an enchanting question: "What do I want to do with this gift?"

I'm here to tell you the answer to this question is, "Anything YOU want!" This is the ultimate beauty of loving yourself unconditionally. One BIG thing you can do when you tap into the unlimited power of self-love is to use it as the centerpiece for defining or redefining your life purpose.

For example, I discovered that I had a gift that enabled me to leverage the power of therapeutic journaling to mitigate my MS symptoms. This realization motivated me to redefine my purpose in life. I made it my mission to show people around the world how they, too, could transform their lives through the healing power of journaling.

In chapter two, I guided you through a process by which you could discover or rediscover your hidden gifts and talents. In subsequent chapters, I've illustrated how to use mindset medicine to nurture and support you gifts, talents, and beliefs with unwavering self-love.

As you and I wind down our journey here together, I want you to tie together everything you've discovered about your-self and write about your new life vision. To do this I'm going to lead you straight into your final journaling prompt.

Your Journaling Power Prompt

This journaling prompt is fun because it allows you to define your purpose, dream big, and go on a beautiful journey.

Throughout this book I've detailed how your life can change if you do the work needed to love yourself and tap into your hidden gifts and talents.

Now I'd like you to think of your gifts and your purpose as a large beautiful crystal that you're about to toss into a shimmering body of water. When you do this, it's going to create an expansive ripple. This is what's going to happen when you realize your purpose and share your gifts with the world.

Yes, if you want to you can create a ripple effect that has a global impact! You can also choose to create a ripple effect that's limited to your local community. It's up to you, because we're talking about YOUR gifts and YOUR purpose—fueled by your unconditional self-love.

The point of this journaling prompt is to paint a picture with words that illustrates what your ripple effect looks like. I also want you to describe to whom it impacts. In short, grab your pen and pad, and create an image of what the world looks like now that you're living your purpose and sharing your gifts.

Is your purpose saving dogs and supporting a local rescue organization? If so, how are you helping this rescue? Who have you met? How many dogs have you saved? How is your community benefiting from your efforts?

Paint this picture in vivid detail!

Have you awakened your passion for writing? Are you writing short stories on the side and sharing them through a blog you've created? If so, what are your stories about? Who is reading them? Who are you engaging with online that otherwise you wouldn't have met? Are you building a fan base of readers? How fulfilling and satisfying is this for you?

Create this world in your journal and bring it to life!

Go on a peaceful mental journey and describe in detail the transformation that is occurring in your world, because you love yourself enough to step up and share your gifts and your purpose with others.

Let your writing flow. Paint pictures with your words. Define your purpose with crystal-clear clarity. Fuel your writing with emotion. Soar through your world as if you have complete and total command over its magnificent creation—because you do!

Have fun with this. Be childlike with your imagination. Let loose and go for it.

Most of all, enjoy your journey. Make it an unforgettable journey, and love yourself unconditionally every second you're alive.

Acknowledgments

It takes a lot of dedicated people to bring a book from concept to completion, so I am grateful to everyone who helped me develop *Mindset Medicine* and bring it to life.

First, I'd like to acknowledge the amazing members of my *Create Write Now* tribe who fill me with gratitude and inspiration every day of my life. It is truly a gift to be able to interact online and in person with such a tremendous gathering of like-minded souls.

In addition, I'd like to thank and acknowledge Copywriter & Consultant Casey Demchak for his assistance in the development of this book and its marketing content.

I'd also like to thank Lawrence O'Brien at *www.Books-GoSocial.com* who was instrumental in publishing this book.

Lastly, I'd like to thank all of my fellow revolutionaries who have the courage to grab a pen and a pad, open their hearts and minds, and just write!

You're all part of a growing movement that is having a tremendous ripple effect throughout the world.

You can help make the ripple bigger by visiting my tribe: *www.CreateWriteNow.com.*

About Mari L. McCarthy

"Through the therapeutic power of journaling I discovered, uncovered, and recovered my True Self, and even tapped into talents I never knew I had."

In 1998, I lost the feeling and function in the right side of my body. Multiple Sclerosis (MS) took them from me. The doctors and all of the prescription drugs they were giving me weren't really helping, so I began a journey to take control of my health.

It wasn't easy for me. I had to learn to write with my left hand. But I dedicated myself to daily ACTION and began a journaling practice known as Morning Pages. I never could have anticipated how powerful and effective this process would become.

As I continued my writing practice, my MS symptoms improved. In fact, because of journaling I was able to ditch my prescription drugs and mitigate most of my symptoms.

Even more important, through journaling I discovered, uncovered, and recovered my True Self and even tapped into talents I never knew I had.Best of all, I developed a compassionate relationship with myself and an inner serenity.

I started *CreateWriteNow* to share my methods, expertise, and passion for my *Journaling For The Health Of It*™ with people across the globe who want to master their life challenges and thrive.

I'd love to see you join our revolution.

Think you can't do this? Well I'm here to tell you that you can. Because remember, the only right way to journal is YOUR way!"

Mari L. McCarthy –
Professional Background

Mari L. McCarthy is the Founder and Chief Empowerment Officer of **Create Write Now**. She is also an international best-selling author of the books, **Journaling Power: How to Create the Happy, Healthy Life You Want to Live,** and **Heal Yourself with Journaling Power.**

In addition, Mari is the creator of 20+ Journaling For The Health Of It® eWorkbooks that have had a life-changing impact on countless people around the world.

Mari lives in a gorgeous beachfront home in Boston, where she has the freedom, flexibility and physical ability to indulge in all of her passions.

In fact, you'll usually find her writing, singing, reading, walking the beach, meditating, practicing photography, cheering on the Pittsburgh Steelers, and raising roses and consciousness!

Before uncovering her true self through the power of journaling, Mari never dreamed she could become a singer.

Well, goodbye to limits! In 2015 she released her **third** album, *Lady With a Song*, and she is currently working on her fourth album.

Mari literally created ALL of this through *Journaling Power.* She now lives life on HER terms, and she is passionately dedicated to helping people around the globe do the same.

You can continue your journey with Mari by staying in touch with her online. She'd love to hear your *Journaling Power* transformation story and your thoughts on the journaling tools and insights she shares through her blog, books, and instructional programs.

Connecting with Mari is easy.

Join the Journaling Power Revolution!

www.CreateWriteNow.com
YouTube.com/c/CreateWriteNow
Facebook.com/CreateWriteNow

Mari L. McCarthy's Journaling Power Workbooks

Self-Healing Courses
- Love Your Body in 28 Days
- Ease Life's Transitions in 22 Days
- 15 Days of Care for the Caregiver
- 7 Steps To Heal Your Grief
- 15 Days Spiritual Journey
- Empower Your Self
- Start Journaling For The Health Of It™ Write Now

Self-Development Courses
- Money Mastery in 7 Days
- Set Better Goals in 7 Days
- Turn Passion into A Career in 7 Days
- Reset & Recharge Your Life in 7 Days
- Take Control Of Your Health in 24 Days
- Declutter Your Life in 21 Days
- Change Your Life in 15 Days

Self-Growth Courses
- Heal Your Life In 27 Days
- Who Am I?
- Detox Your Relationships in 14 Days
- Fun Filled Holidays in 7 Days
- Discover Your True Self in 23 Days

Courses for Writers

- 53 Weekly Writing Retreats
- 14 Days of Journal Magic for Writers
- 12 Day Guide to Morning Pages
- Overcome Page Fright in 7 Days
- Build A Lasting Journaling Practice in 14 Days